PERFORMANCE
PUBLISHING

HERMANA,
I WANT TO HEAR YOUR STORY!

Recipes and Testimonies from
Mujeres Nuevo Comienzo

Lisa Costa and Emily Giesbrecht

HERMANA,
I WANT TO HEAR YOUR STORY!

"This book is a powerful testimony of real-life heroes who have navigated through hardship and trial to see the goodness of God made tangible for hurting women and children. *"Hermana, I Want to Hear Your Story"* is a beautiful collection of such stories. Personally, I have had the privilege of seeing firsthand the unconditional love of God poured out through the ministry of Mujeres Nuevo Comienzo. This book is a small collection of the many lives that have been forever changed by the compassion and care expressed daily through this amazing group of people at Mujeres Nuevo Comienzo.

The power of these stories and the mind-blowing revelation of God's astounding provision and grace make this book a must-read. Rarely do we get to see such sacrificial love and unwavering commitment to the mission of Jesus expressed in such a vivid way. I am proud to celebrate and promote these amazing people's incredible work and the bravery displayed by telling these stories. Buckle up; this book will capture your heart."

Tim Fortin
Lead Pastor, River Valley Church

"Hermana, I Want to Hear Your Story!" is a profoundly moving testament to resilience and compassion, weaving personal experiences with the impactful mission of Mujeres Nuevo Comienzo. Lisa and Emily's dedication to making a difference, collaborative efforts in bringing the project to life, and the portrayal of unwavering commitment showcases the transformative power of community and the hope that arises from collective action. The book's thoughtful approach, from trigger warnings to celebrating victories beautifully captures the essence of Mujeres Nuevo Comienzo, offering readers a compelling narrative of strength and empowerment and using the Hispanic culture and delicious recipes that bring us together to enjoy."

Dr. Rosalinda Gallegos Main, DC, CFMP
Owner of Main Health Solutions and author of
bestselling recipe book on Amazon,"*Dr. Rosie's MexiKeto Kitchen*"

"Reading '*Hermana, I Want to Hear Your Story!*' brought to mind the Apostle Paul's epistle to the Galatians: "We know the work of the flesh is obvious—hatred, jealousy, envy, outburst of anger—people who practice these things will not inherit God's Kingdom. But the fruits of the Spirit are love, joy, peace, kindness, faith, gentleness, and self-control—let us walk in the Spirit." (Gal. 5:19-26).

There is evil everywhere. We must be intentional about walking in the Spirit. Reading this book brought me full circle—from heart-wrenching sadness to acknowledging the overwhelming joy of God's grace flowing through the people who serve Him. Lisa and Emily have produced a must-read masterpiece."

Dr. Nathanial Hearne
President and Founder, Euless Loaves and Fishes Foundation and
Author of "*Friday Night Lights: Untold Stories from Behind the Lights*"

"Hermana, I Want to Hear Your Story" is a beautiful and heartfelt cookbook that goes beyond mere recipes; it tells the profound stories of resilience, hope, and transformation in the Mujeres Nuevo Comienzo community. I am honored to support this project and bring these powerful stories to life. This cookbook is a beacon of hope, showcasing the healing power of love, community, and good food."

Michelle Prince
CEO, Performance Publishing
www.PerformancePublishingGroup.com

CONTENTS

I will go before you and will level the mountains;

I will break down gates of bronze and cut through bars of iron.

I will give you hidden treasures, riches stored in secret places,

so that you may know that I am the Lord,

the God of Israel, who summons you by name.

For the sake of Jacob my servant, of Israel my chosen,

I summon you by name and bestow on you a title of honor,

though you do not acknowledge me.

I am the Lord, and there is no other; apart from me there is no God.

I will give you hidden treasures, riches stored in secret places, so that you may know that I am the Lord THE GOD OF ISRAEL who summons you by name

Isaiah 45:3

I will strengthen you, though you have not acknowledged me,

so that from the rising of the sun to the place of its setting

people may know there is none besides me.

I am the Lord, and there is no other.

I form the light and create darkness,

I bring prosperity and create disaster;

I, the Lord, do all these things.

Isaiah 45:2-7 (NIV)

Introduction from the Authors

Emily

My first time hearing about Mujeres Nuevo Comienzo was when I was 15. My family and some others from our local church in Fort St. John B.C. were in Vicente Guerrero, Mexico, building houses with Youth with a Mission (YWAM). One evening, we split up into two groups to go visit different ministries. I was randomly sent to Mujeres Nuevo Comienzo, where we were greeted with spicy jelly, cream cheese, crackers, and testimonies.

These testimonies stuck with me, and my heart was moved with compassion to help. Dorothy shared how MNC came to be and the need for this ministry in Baja California. My parents were there with me, and we all had the burning desire to return and serve here.

A year later, my whole family came back for two weeks during spring break. We painted, cooked, built relationships, sewed, baked, and fell even more in love with what God was doing at MNC. Fast forward five years: my husband and I were newly married and looking for a place to serve during our first year of marriage. Every door we tried to walk through slammed shut until Dorothy arrived in Fort St. John. She pulled me in for a hug and said, "I have a place for you two prepared, just come." So we did. We drove down the California coast in an old motorhome we purchased for this trip and stayed for six months: six life-changing months.

One of my jobs while I was in Vicente Guerrero was catching up on some administrative duties where I heard a recipe/testimony book was in the works, but all the information needed to be gathered for it. It seemed simple enough, and it was a job I could help with.

What I didn't anticipate was the countless hours of interviewing women, recording their stories, grocery shopping, creating their favorite recipes, and documenting them. Those would become precious memories forever locked away in my heart. We cried together and reflected over and over again on how our God is a God who can restore very broken and hopeless situations.

Yours is no exception. Our prayer over this book is as you flip through these pages the Holy Spirit will reveal to you His faithfulness and bring awareness of how we can help put an end to sex trafficking and abuse. He has restored so many of these women who would have told you they had nothing left. He is still moving and working in the lives of some of my dear friends at Mujeres Nuevo Comienzo. I feel blessed to have had the opportunity and to be a piece in putting this beautiful book together.

Lisa

I have had the amazing opportunity to be a part of more than a dozen mission and service projects in my life, and I am looking forward to many, many more. One trip that captured my heart immediately was the one on which I met Dorothy, the woman who answered the call she heard from God to create the mission.

Our group was staying at a local orphanage, and we went to visit other missions in the area. We had a short tour of the small mission: a few buildings, multiple travel trailers being used as makeshift housing for the women and children staying there for refuge, and a tarp-covered area with multiple folding tables where we sat and learned about Mujeres Nuevo Comienzo (MNC).

As Dorothy greeted our group with Texas sheet cake and jalapeño jelly on Ritz crackers, I welled up with tears. My grandmother, whom I had loved dearly, had recently passed away and Texas sheet cake was a treat she would commonly make for us. At the end of each September, we would indulge in her jalapeño jelly on Ritz crackers! I believe God puts us in the right place at the right time, just when our hearts need it most. Dorothy reminds me of my grandmother in many ways, one of which is their shared heartfelt drive to make sure life continues for their loved ones through difficult circumstances.

As we continued with the tour, Dorothy told of the horrific stories of the women who come to MNC. Not only was my stomach in knots with disgust at how they had been treated, but there was a tug on my heart where I asked God, "How can I help?" The feeling never went away. I don't believe it was a coincidence I met this woman shortly after my grandmother left this earth.

When I arrived home, I taped a picture of Dorothy to my workspace and prayed for her mission for the next year. I asked to be part of the planning committee for the following year, when our group would visit. I helped organize and plan to get as much done as humanly possible in the four short days we would be there.

God met us in our cry, and we accomplished much more than we even thought possible. In four days, the team installed three bathrooms with tile; painted five large cinder block rooms (primer and paint); installed 450 square feet of vinyl flooring; completed a clothing room for the ladies and children with shelving; fixed electrical problems; painted two large murals; played with the children; held multiple nutrition and self-care classes; provided a vacation Bible school for the MNC children and the community children, and built a home for a woman with three children transitioning out of MNC to live on their own. Only by the grace of God were these labors of love possible.

After our successful visit, the shelter was still heavy on my heart. "What else can I do, God?" My family of seven is a middle-class working family with little money to spare, but we have a heart to serve. I felt led in the direction of building relationships in the community of Vicente Guerrero. My next assignment was to maintain contact with special people I had been blessed to get to meet during our trips. I found cheap flights for a January trip and took three of my kids back for an extended weekend.

Then I thought, "I can't consistently send as much money as she needs to support the mission... but I can help fundraise." This book was born. In July of 2022, I attended a conference and sitting next to me just happened to be the owner of Prince Publishing. I shared Dorothy's story with Michelle Prince, and she felt inspired to be part of the project too.

I had been considering how to bring this book to life for several months when I met Emily on another January trip to Dorothy's. She and her husband were living there for several months as long-term volunteers. She was as excited about the project as I was and took on the huge task of collecting the recipes and testimonies of the ladies. Our gracious God, the Architect of this project, brought together the right people stretching from Canada to the United States (Idaho to Florida) and to Mexico to work on this project.

I am thrilled to contribute to a project that may provide a long-term source of income for Mujeres Nuevo Comienzo! There are many more women needing refuge and training. Helping support the longevity of this mission is part of my own mission. Thank you for joining in support. Also, thank you to the hundreds of volunteers who have helped and continue to help MNC's journey to provide healing for women, the children, and a community, and ultimately leaving a legacy of change.

Trigger Warning

The next portion of this book is a series of testimonies from past and current (Spring 2023) residents of Mujeres Nuevo Comienzo. We do not recommend that children under 13 should read this book; parental guidance is advised. Be prepared for a series of stories that may shock and sadden you. Many of the stories contain narratives of women who have experienced various forms of abuse. The stories shared within may include descriptions of physical, emotional, psychological, and/or sexual abuse, and could be triggering or distressing for some readers.

It is important to prioritize your well-being while engaging with this material. If you have a history of trauma or are currently struggling with your mental health, please stop to consider whether reading the testimonies is the right choice for you. If you do choose to read, we recommend doing so in a supportive environment and reaching out to a mental health professional or a trusted person if you need emotional support.

This is a very heavy read for sadness and joy. There are many stories of healing and hope that have come from this mission; the ladies at MNC are similar to women around the world who experience trauma. For many women, it's easier to go back to the known than to face the scary unknown of healing; they often have yet to discover their own value. Not all women have the success of growing to better lives, or what we would see as success stories. For some, their stay at MNC was the short breath they needed for rest and to see compassion and love. Let's remember to celebrate these successes too.

The recipes in this book are from the ladies themselves. Emily took them to the store to gather their ingredients, wrote down the recipe as they cooked, and translated it for this book. These are their methods and ingredients.

Many of the names and pictures of the residents and former resident ladies have been changed to protect their identities. Some pictures next to testimonies are stock images.

As you read through the testimonies, you'll see many of the ladies saying, "Thank you!" They truly appreciate all the help and support that has made it possible for them to have a better chance in life.

Welcome to Mujeres Nuevo Comienzo

Sitting on the top of a hill, in Baja California, outside of the village of Vicente Guerrero, is a ministry that never sleeps. Silence is an uncommon occurrence here. Children play and holler, moms are busy with their daily responsibilities, the dogs bark, roosters crow, and a constant environment of busy-ness keeps everyone on the move. Mujeres Nuevo Comienzo (MNC) is a ministry orchestrated by God. A dream of creating a women's center was birthed in an old lady's heart nearly 20 years ago. In 2011, at the age of 70, Dorothy filled out the application to the Mexican government to open MNC. Her dream was to provide a safe home for women who have been victims of sexual abuse and domestic violence. Dorothy saw the horrors of young girls being jailed for prostitution, when the reality was, they were being sex trafficked against their will. She saw young moms in the community beaten and battered with no other option for starting a new life than leaving her children with the abuser or at an orphanage while trying to heal and find employment and housing. Loosely translated, the name Mujeres Nuevo Comienzo means 'New Beginning for Women', which is exactly what happens at MNC.

Healing within a context of loneliness and abandonment is near impossible for those who are experiencing abuse. At the shelter, they don't have to live life alone any longer. It's a home where women and their children can heal together and dream about their future in a safe and caring environment. The women are encouraged and empowered to pursue restoration. Dorothy calls the ministry a place where ladies get to make a choice: a choice to heal and pick their future path, not continue down a path chosen for them. Since the doors opened in 2012, MNC has been an answer to prayer for many, providing missing resources for women who desire to transform their lives.

It is not just a place to lay their heads at night without retribution; the home helps women discover their value and their purpose in life – a place that cultivates their confidence. The shelter offers a place of respite and protection similar to the cocoon for a caterpillar. The safety gives the women an opportunity to restructure and grow, where they can choose to emerge as a new life. The beautiful symbolism can be seen on many walls and halls of MNC. Butterflies are painted throughout as peaceful reminders of hope and freedom. As you read the women's testimonies in this book, watch for the metamorphosis of their butterfly wings. Their redemption is characterized by the resilience and strength exhibited from choosing to go through the process to emerge as survivors of the harrowing abuse they endured. These women have experienced power from God to work within themselves, with loving support and care, to emerge from their past traumas as new, stronger, brilliant creations ready to take flight.

Dorothy, lovingly referred to as Abuela (Grandmother), daily petitions God for His will to be done at MNC. Those prayers are visibly answered in their day-to-day life and years later in the testimonies of women and children who have experienced healing there. A great increase in financial and missionary support over the last six years, provides resources for counseling, tutoring, and occasionally medical and dental care. The ministry has many helpers who supply building maintenance and those who offer their time to help with the overall daily operations or support the mission through prayers from afar.

Depending on the day, Abuela and some of the residents collaboratively work in the bakery kitchen processing raspberries, baking cookies, or canning jelly. Abuela enjoys the opportunity to build relationships and learn more about them, asking questions like, "What do you want to do? What are your dreams?" Often, their biggest dreams are limited to working in the berry fields. Abuela constantly encourages the ladies to dream bigger, "Want to be an engineer? Doctor? Teacher? Let's find a way to make it happen!" Women find more than a refuge at MNC; they find a future. While at the ministry, they learn to cook with proper sanitation, decorate cakes, preserve food with canning, make sausages, sew, garden, and care for animals. Dorothy hopes to add a hair salon for another vocational opportunity soon.

The women are also encouraged to gain work experience in a meaningful field through local internships and job placements. MNC has an on-site restaurant, Buen Provecho, and recently added a café (coffee shop) upstairs with a breathtaking view of the valley and the ocean. These provide another training environment for them to gain skills in hospitality, cashiering, waitressing, and cooking. The restaurant and café are open to the public, with safeguards in place, allowing the residents to maintain safety.

Earning money is a valuable and needed skill. Dorothy also donates her time to teach them how to manage money and to think about future needs. With the money they earn, she encourages them to save, tithe, and invest in property so they can someday build a home.

Dorothy highly values the volunteers who come to MNC. She invites volunteers into a relationship when they visit. For me, when I visit MNC I will usually find myself in the bakery with Dorothy, helping make cookies or sorting vegetables. Many good conversations happen in the bakery. When Dorothy discovers a volunteer or a resident has a special talent, she often pairs it with a need at the ministry, inviting them to be part of the MNC story. The logo is one of those stories; it is a beautiful expression of hope, healing, and transformation. It was designed by a teenage girl who grew up with a drug-addicted mother.

Often the children of drug-addicted and abused mothers become a product of their environment, growing up damaged and becoming victims as well. This logo demonstrates what happens to children when they are subjected to living and growing up in this type of environment. The large tree represents the mother with her arms held high surrendering to God. When she surrenders, the fruit takes hold in the children's lives. The branches on the left, center, and bottom right are her three children who are clinging to their mother's legs. The one on the left with flourishing leaves has come out of the darkness and is doing well. The one in the center bottom is really struggling and is hiding in the darkness. The one on the bottom right with no leaves, is struggling in the same way, but is making a sincere effort to come out of the darkness. The one at the very top right with flourishing leaves is the pregnant mother with a baby in her womb.

There are many murals and art pieces around the ministry. Dorothy uses many illustrations when talking about the importance of the ministry. In the Summer of 2022, she made a request to a group of volunteers asking them to paint on the side of the two-story building a large teapot, big enough to be seen from the highway, pouring into a teacup.

She says, "Tea pots are a touch of elegance, hope, and comfort." The pouring out symbolizes the care of inviting those who have an empty cup to experience the knowledge others have gained along their journey. It's important to be willing to share and help bring hope and comfort to others.

A commonly asked question is: how do women come to stay at the ministry? Some are brought by police – removed from a crisis situation in the middle of the night with none of their belongings or clothes, brought to the mission as they are. Women can also call directly asking for help. If someone can safely pick them up, arrangements are made, or a family member can bring them, or sometimes the women find a way to get there themselves.

To stay at the ministry, a few requirements must be met. The first requirement is to have need for a safe place away from abuse, neglect, human trafficking, sexual abuse, etc. Second, they cannot have a phone or be in contact with anyone who does not go through Dorothy, Susie (the onsite house mother), or Jorge (the office manager). This is for their own safety and the safety of the residents at MNC. Third, they will have devotions, chores, recreational activities, and life skills training, and they will have to cook their own meals. After three months, the women can start to work and eventually save up to put a payment on a piece of land and pay it off as time allows.

After they secure property, they can apply for a home to be built by a mission team, such as YWAM or Student Reach. A process is in place where they meet with a legal team and are interviewed to ensure they meet the requirements of a house blessing. These requirements include: the woman cannot already own another house, the property she's purchasing must be in her name (in case she gets married, she cannot lose it if the spouse tries to evict her), and she must show stability and the ability to maintain a home. Once an application is accepted, the woman goes on a list for multiple missions in the area. It is common for women who are leaving MNC to receive a house before they leave or while they are living in transition housing.

Other women in the area can apply for housing as well. Many times, those families have built what is called a "plastic house" on the property they buy while waiting for their turn on a house list. The plastic house is normally comprised of black tarps tied to posts to create a home-like structure with outside walls and a cover over the top. Imagine a box made of plastic that still leaks when it rains, and the walls move when the wind blows. Women are not able to stay at MNC if they have teenage boys, but staff will find alternative housing in those circumstances. Investments are not common here, but property is a good investment, so the women are encouraged to buy their own. A local businessman works with the women to choose a lot and assumes the debt. The women then make payments until the property is paid in full. When the full amount has been paid, the businessman transfers the ownership to them. They are also encouraged to tithe and give.

MNC's Programs

0-3 months

No cell phone or contact with outside people unless permission is obtained or it's important to their journey. Children are required to attend school. Women are responsible for keeping their areas tidy and caring for their children.

3-6 months

If the woman is finding healing, is emotionally stable, and physically fit, then MNC staff will help them find a job. They can work on site at the ministry or in the community to earn wages. They are also encouraged to tithe and give.

6-12 months

The ministry will help with childcare when the mom is working. Women are still expected to care for their living area and assist with chores on site.

After 1 year

When they are ready to live on their own, MNC has four transition houses for women to live with their children. This helps them practice independence while still having assistance and accountability. Sometimes, they are ready for transition housing before the one year milestone. They must care for the home and continue to go to church. Most stay there until they receive a home if they have applied and been approved from a local home-build ministry. Other times they find another home to live in.

MNC's Programs

8:00 am

Women prepare their breakfast every weekday.

On the weekends Dorothy will make them pancakes or a special breakfast. Devotions with Susie, the house mom, or a local pastor. Chores take place throughout the day.

12:00 pm

Women rotate cooking and cleaning up from lunch. Sometimes other activities are available like baking, sewing, biking, walks, canning, painting, crafts, etc. There is a counselor who schedules visits during this time. Onsite daycare is available until 2:00 pm. After that moms are to take care of their children and spend time with them.

5:00 pm

Women rotate cooking and cleaning up from dinner. Kids are asked to be put to bed after dinner and ladies can stay up and visit until bedtime.

9:30 pm Lights out

On the weekends staff work to arrange fun outings like hiking or beach days depending on the number of volunteers available.

History of Mujeres Nuevo Comienzo

2011

In October of 2011 Dorothy filed the paperwork to open the AC (a government recognized civil association) similar to a non-profit status. On the 17th of December they moved into an old orphanage and began extensive repairs.

2012

On the 4th of April they cut the ribbon and opened the doors. It was small, needed work, but no woman was turned away.

2015

In 2015 the ministry put a deposit down on a 2.5-acre lot. She envisioned a much larger facility to help more people. Improvements on the current property continued to allow for more growth.

2017

On the 20th of December Mujeres Nuevo Comienzo moved to the new property. It was all but bare with one structure that served as a tool shed. A local businessman donated a bus, another donated a travel trailer and the local Youth With a Mission (YWAM) donated 8 tents to the mission.

2018

This was a very busy year. With many donors and volunteers, the ministry built a fence for safety, a water storage building, and a two-story building with kitchen/dining on the ground floor and a sleeping area and prayer room above. The bus was converted into a sewing room, while more travel trailers and a shed were donated. A fenced-in, tented outdoor space was built, as was a small greenhouse.

2019

The projects continued and finishing touches were added with functioning bathrooms, paint, flooring, and electrical. They broke ground for a large 10,000 square foot facility; two stories and plenty of room for the residents to live and play. Also, included in the blueprints were a restaurant and cafe to provide training for residents and an income for the mission.

2020

As you can imagine, this year was a much slower year due to the emergence of the COVID pandemic. The borders were closed, stopping volunteers from coming. Schools were shut down and children had to be educated on-site. Building slowed and came to a stop for some time. The border remained closed until spring of 2021.

2023

The building has grown and daily nearing completion daily. The ministry made a down payment on an adjoining 2.5-acre lot, anticipating continued growth of the ministry. The next building project is to build housing units for volunteers to stay while working at MNC.

Statistics of Mujeres Nuevo Comienzo

7
Most children one mother has brought with her

11
Most women at one time living at MNC

23
Women living independently in house builds

400
Residents over 12 years

10,000
Monthly cost to operate

10,500
Average monthly donations

5
Acreage of MNC

19
Structures

1,000+
Volunteers over 12 years

The monthly operating costs of Mujeres Nuevo Comienzo on average total $10,000 dollars. This does not include project building materials or the unexpected expenses of a car breaking down or a child getting sick. The $10,000 budget is purely for basic care and operating costs. Without generous donations and miracles, MNC would not be where it is today.

Many miracles have taken place that allow MNC to operate to its fullest capacity. Unexpected gifts of stoves; refrigerators; vehicles; building supplies and materials; food; design and engineering expertise; content creators; carpenters...the list goes on. There have been some incredible people who have led large fundraisers to generate funds that have moved large building projects forward. It is miraculous how many people come to MNC, realize they have a talent, and choose to use their talent to grow the ministry.

Has a Life Been Changed?

"No Numbers!"

As I sat with Dorothy jotting notes, listening to her recount story after story of different ladies who have visited the center, I asked her how many had come to reside at MNC. She quickly replied, "If a life has been changed, I don't care about the numbers." She then clarified: "It's about a life being changed." This adamancy reminded me of the starfish story: As an adolescent walked the beach filled with starfish brought in from the tide, the child picked one up and threw it back into the ocean, took another step, and tossed another. An adult scoffed, asking what difference they thought it would make with hundreds scattered about. The child reached down for another, gave a gentle toss, and said "I made a difference for that one."

In a similar way, Dorothy knows there are hundreds if not thousands suffering and needing help, but those numbers don't discourage her or stop her from making a difference for another. She knows she can only help as many as she has room and funding for, so she continues to reach out with needs and provides people an opportunity to be part of the ministry with her. She has never turned a lady away due to lack of space. She has found "corners and blankets" for anyone needing solace.

It is the woman's choice to stay as long as she abides by the agreed upon rules. Dorothy has only asked one to leave, which saddened her deeply. The lady was causing so much dissension, it was disrupting the living environment for the other ladies and children, so she felt she had no choice but to ask her to find another place to stay.

Daily, Dorothy continues to fight for more opportunities for the ladies living at MNC, helps past residents pay bills when they face hardship, and gives out food and clothes when people express need or if she knows a need exists. She prays continuously. Although not all choose to stay and get the help they need, Dorothy chooses to plant a seed of care, love, and hope for whatever the length of time may be. Only God knows what impact the seed will have. What makes it possible for MNC to continue this support? It's possible because Dorothy is a woman who lives in prayer, persistence, and passion – a passion to provide opportunities to change lives and generations of families.

Even though she doesn't keep count of all who come to stay, Jorge (the office manager) does. As of July 2023, over 400 ladies have resided at MNC. Some choose to stay for a few years, some just for one night. One week in July while I was there, two ladies were brought in by the Purple Squad (the police who specialize in women's care) and two were brought in by a family member. In less than 24 hours, all chose to leave and go back to the life from which they were brought in.

The mission has a one-year program for the residents designed in stages to help give the participants the best launch toward living a life of choice. As I sat across the table from Dorothy and a businessman from the valley, he asked, "What do you do here?" I chuckled, thinking to myself, What don't you do? Smiling at me and then back at him, she explained that she provides a home for women to finally have a choice. Her tone changed to one more somber, but direct, as she emphasized that the ladies who come here never had a choice in the life they formerly lived; instead, they had been forced to endure many hardships with no hope for escape.

Coming to the ministry means they now get the great opportunity to hear they are valuable, they were created for a purpose, and they are loved. Most women come with little to no self-esteem or sense of self-worth. She recited Isaiah 45:3 (NKJV), which says, "I will give you the treasures of darkness and hidden riches of secret places, that you may know that I, the Lord, Who calls you by your name, Am the God of Israel."

The journey is different for each resident. Sadly, it isn't uncommon for some to stay only a few short nights or weeks. Many ladies are brought in during the evening and leave within days of their arrival. For the first three months of the program, participants are allowed no cell phones or contact with people outside of the ministry. This helps them recalibrate and break free from the previous living condition and helps them create new habits. For some, this is extremely difficult, and for others, a welcome peace.

In a world of instant contact and communication coupled with exiting a traumatic lifestyle, it is a hard adjustment. Imagine living most of your life in fear, rejection, and depletion while learning to cope and survive. The trauma from the abuse that has occurred can have many negative effects on the body. Additional pressure to stay in their situation comes when there are people relying on them for care or service. From a very young age, many of the residents MNC helps have never experienced a sense of self-worth or an understanding of having intrinsic value. If one does not believe they are valuable, what would the justification for fighting for better treatment be?

Lacking self-worth can lead to many unhealthy lifestyle choices. This can build a deep-rooted shame and people-pleasing tendencies. Ellen Brown talks about trauma and notes its effects impacting our mental and physical health, employment, education, crime, relationships, domestic or family abuse, alcoholism, and drug addiction. Trauma can disrupt our neurochemistry, which explains how hard it can be for the women coming to the mission to leave the trap of abuse behind. They have been beaten

The illiterate around the world:

- earn 35% less than their literate counterparts
- often face welfare dependency
- have lower self-esteem
- commit higher levels of crime
- exhibit lower ability to make important decisions
- struggle with tasks such as filling out forms and applications
- have difficulty reading medicine or nutritional labels
- as parents, are less likely to help their children pursue education, which perpetuates the cycle
- are more likely to experience poor health and practice poor health behaviors
- have higher hospital admission rates
- experience a lack of preventative health services such as cancer screening
- World Literacy Foundation; Berkman et al. (2004)

down emotionally, mentally, and or physically for several years. They may feel undeserving, or they may fear repercussions for what will happen if they are gone too long.

The body and brain will go to great lengths to protect us, including detaching itself from numb, painful memories to protect us from further abuse. It is also common for the abused to protect their abuser. Dorothy mentioned how often the girls protect their abuser as she shared a story of a small teenager, who was around age 13 when she first came to the MNC. Her mother tried to escape the abuse in her life and came to the ministry with the 13-year-old and several of her siblings. The girl would not talk to anyone. She stayed curled up in the fetal position and hid for hours. She was anxiety-ridden and her emotional unrest would torment her so ferociously that she pulled her hair out of her head, leaving bloody bald spots on her scalp. The mother and her children only stayed a few months, and she then took the family back to the home (and the abuse) they knew. This small, distressed teen came back to MNC at 15, pregnant with her first child and looking for hope. Her testimony is in this book, but she never mentions the part of her story that included her mother telling her at just nine years old she was going to start spending time with her uncle, and to allow him to do as he pleased to help pay the bills. Nor does she share about the many other abusers she met at the hands of her mother.

Another unsettling number for those not accustomed to the culture on the Baja is that out of the 400 women who have come to MNC, fewer than 20 have more than a third-grade level of education. This means reading and writing in their own language is not common. Illiteracy can lead to even more life disadvantages. Dorothy's goal is to help women and their children read and write while they are staying at the mission. Stopping the cycle is the way to empower true life change and create a ripple effect to change the community.

Not only do the ladies have a disadvantage when it comes to reading and writing, but some also don't even speak the official Spanish language. There are several indigenous languages spoken in the area. It might be shocking to some of those reading this, but there is a large amount of racism in the villages. Two tribes in particular are considered a minority and are the ones commonly abused and taken advantage of. These tribes are frequently exploited as slaves to farmers or to sex trafficking rings. Some are treated poorly in the villages and refused services, education, and/or employment.

The Oaxacan tribe is one that is frequently exploited by local farms for cheap labor, is enslaved in tiny camps if they don't have their own housing and become indebted to their landlord. Living in these depressive and hopeless environments can lead to abuse of drugs and alcohol because they are cheap and readily accessible coping methods. Their children become targets of human traffickers, either snatching them or convincing a family they are providing them with a better life if they consent to giving them up.

Every story may be different, but the pain and anguish are so similar. On one visit I made to Dorothy's House, I met a lady who was about my age – early forties. She approached me and handed me a rock she had found on her walk hours before; she said God moved her to give the rock to me (yes, I still have it). I was surprised at how good her English was. As we talked more and shared stories, we discovered we grew up less than 70 miles from each other in the States. She recounted times of drug use with her father starting around 11 years old. Her family was involved in dealing drugs and some carried ties to organized drug distributors. Her life was a crazy roller coaster from jail to sobriety to marriage as a teen to a 30-plus-year-old man, to prison, to being deported back to Mexico. After deportation, she maintained sobriety for over 10 years living a typical "suburban family" life in Mexico. Eventually, a small itch for the dopamine hit started and a new boyfriend encouraged recreational use, which then took her life on a drastic turn back to drugs.

For the next several years she was in and out of rehabilitation treatment centers. When the police found her strung out in the streets, they would take her to a nearby center. One time in rehab, a roommate told her about MNC and her dreams of going to the safe haven. The new friend asked her to meet her there once they were able to leave the facility. One night she "escaped" and went on a journey to find her boyfriend. Upon reunion, an uncommon event occurred, and he severely beat, kicked, and bit her. Caught off guard, she was shocked and struggled to flee for her life. After escaping the beating, she wandered through the streets in a stupor, begging for a hit to ease the pain and confusion. A man on a motorcycle stopped and provided what she was looking for. He then took her to his pastor's home for prayer. The pastor helped her find her way down the Baja to Dorothy's mission.

When we met, her face was still marred with bruises and teeth marks. She was incredible to talk to. Her eyes were filled with sadness, regret, and great hope. Her strength astounded me. She had a vigor and excitement to get back to living a life of freedom from drugs and reunite with her children. A few weeks later I reached out to the mission to check on my new friend and she was no longer there. She chose to go back to rehab, but we do not know where she is now. I pray only the best for her.

The journey to a new life can be hard. Many of the women have said they don't know where they would be without this ministry. They have a new family here. They have new "sisters" and people surrounding them who love and care for them. As I talked to other women and read through some testimonies, I can see clearly that the ministry was the positive in-filling they needed to start seeing a tiny sliver of light in the dark tunnel of self-worth.

When multiple people in life constantly tell someone they have no value, it becomes very believable. It's hard to transition to thinking another way when most of one's life has consisted of living out the belief of worthlessness. Dorothy relates to the ladies on so many levels. She has experienced abuse and neglect, hurt and pain from life's choices, and redemption. To help in the women's journey, she speaks love and encouragement but is also able to have real conversations about choices and expectations.

Before she established MNC, Dorothy was working in an orphanage in Vicente Guerro. She had come from Canada on a visa to volunteer in Mexico. During her time at the orphanage, she grew in understanding the local customs and culture as she interacted with the community. She had a deep compassion and empathy as she asked God how to help alleviate their pain and suffering. She desperately wanted to give women a lifelong change, not just a Band-Aid for the pain they had endured. Dorothy did not let her dreams die in her youth. She was 70 and considered an "old lady" when she first filed the papers for MNC. There is no age limit to your life purpose. For as long as you are willing, God can use you.

With age comes experience to help along the way. Not everyone acquires wisdom with age, but those who choose to learn from life's lessons can accumulate great wisdom and grit. Dorothy's journey is an incredible story of determination born of lessons learned. She experienced pain in life and in ministry and she learned to give it to God, living out her belief: "Not my will, but His." Giving worry, stress, and confusion to God releases a peace beyond human understanding. She met a lot of adversity while starting the Mujeres Nuevo Comienzo ministry. Through it, she steadily and daily gave it to God.

In the early days, the ministry consisted of Dorothy and another volunteer. Some local missionaries assisted the start, and the ministry then grew into a great team. The staff included an office manager, house mom, and a few assistants. After making the move to the new property in December of 2017, things began changing. In March of 2018, the staff of MNC tried to remove Dorothy as the director. They made several changes to accounts and diverted donations into a new account, contacted supporters, and got official papers before she knew what was happening. They forced her off the property, leaving her to live in a leaky tent. They went to the extent of campaigning to have her deported back to Canada. She stated, "But God provided, and we survived."

Even though she was stripped of all resources, she continued to serve the needs of women and children who came to the mission. Dorothy said while she was recounting the story, "Whose ministry is it?" The staff was saying it was theirs and not hers. Dorothy says, "It's God's. It's not my ministry; it's not anybody else's; it's God's." The Mexican government stepped in and restored Dorothy as the director of the A.C. (Civil Association). The others left and created their own ministry, which still serves and helps others in the community. Good can come from hardships when we are willing to see the good. The path isn't always easy, nor is it promised to us. Our responsibility is to persevere when we know we are doing what we have been called to do.

A few months after Dorothy was reinstated, MNC received an award from the Mexican government for "Making a Difference in Mexico." That was a pivotal experience for MNC, and the growth began exponentially as a result. YWAM came and built the bakery in July, and other teams came to finish buildings and help with the grounds. In six short years, blessing after blessing flowed into MNC. Donation amounts grew and although they came sporadically, they were timely for the work needing to be done. Over the last six years (2017-2023), MNC has grown from bare land to nearly 20 structures. Dorothy said in our interview it's evident "how small we are and how big God is."

Recipes and Testimonies

Dorothy

Here I am, just past celebrating my 82nd birthday. How did it happen so quickly? When I turn my memories loose, they hop and skip through many different chapters of life. Some include being orphaned, abandoned, rejected, sexually abused, and physically beaten. Above all, I can see a love that has been unstoppable and immeasurable. I remember riding on my daddy's shoulders and his strong hugs. No doubt this solid foundation carried me through the years of loneliness, fear, and frustration.

In one blink of an eye, my parents died in a car accident, taking from me all I had ever known. All nine of my siblings were separated. A lack of healthy role models in my teen years and no comprehension of boundaries plunged me into making dreadful decisions, and I paid for the disastrous results of those choices. My poor choices have included an abortion, divorce, adultery, foul language, and running from my problems instead of addressing them. Somehow, I stand redeemed and completely forgiven. How can this be, He would die for me? Grace and mercy are my choice words since finding Jesus at the age of 59. God has been so patient with me. Sometimes the chipping and polishing hurt deeply, and even though I have had many pity parties and frustrations, He always sends somebody to minister and help me get back on my feet. The people on my journey have been many: a nameless bus driver; an amazing grade nine teacher; an old grandma who gave me daily hugs just when I needed; my sisters Olga and Bernice. There have been many more but even so, I have made dreadful mistakes and terrible choices.

Now in my golden years, I am enjoying a journey of watching unbelievable transformation in women and children who have been rescued from abuse. My own journey looked so shattered and broken but God turned it around so I can confidently say, "Come, let us help you."

Here we have a houseful of broken and abused women. Some days they are attacking each other, and other days they are embracing each other through the hard times. Our mealtime together brings a sense of normality.

Somehow, sharing a meal can bring a totally new rhythm and help us connect with the heartbeat of each other. This recipe book is filled with testimonies of past and present residents who have grasped how wide and long, how high, and deep is the love of Christ. They are learning that His love surpasses all human knowledge. He doesn't see us as dirty vessels; He calls us his own – redeemed. We pray as you go through these testimonies, you will see how God has restored these women even when they felt like their situation was too far gone. Each woman shared their favorite dish, and we hope you enjoy it also.

Blessings,

Dorothy
Founder of Mujeres Nuevo Comienzo

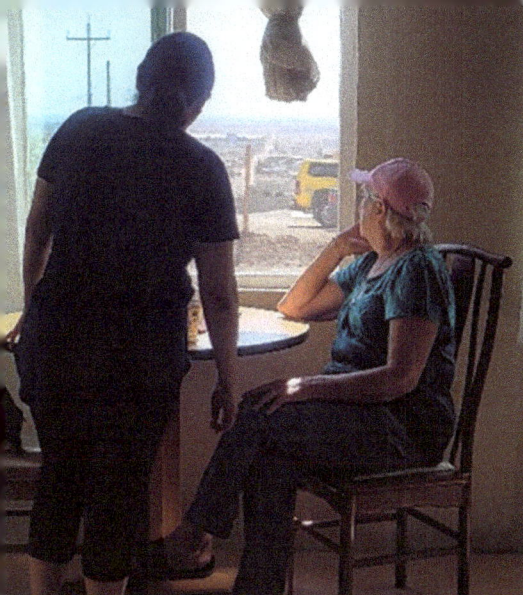

Dorothy's Donuts

Ingredients:

¼ cup warm water
2 tbsp instant yeast
1½ cup warm milk
½ cup sugar
½ tsp salt

⅓ cup shortening
5 cups flour
2 eggs
1 tsp vanilla
3-4 cups oil

Glaze:

4 cups icing sugar
2 tsp vanilla

11 tbsp milk

Directions:

In one bowl, place ¼ cup warm water, 1½ cup warm milk, ½ cup sugar, and 2 tbsp yeast. Allow to sit for 5 minutes.

In a second large mixing bowl, add the rest of the ingredients. Mix well. Once the first bowl has sat for five minutes add the two mixtures together and knead well.

Let rise in a warm place for 15 minutes. Lightly flour the surface and divide dough into equal pieces. Roll into little balls and poke a hole into the middle with your finger. Gently work them from the hole outward into the shape of a donut by stretching and flattening between your hands.

In a pot, heat 3-4 cups of oil of choice. Once oil is hot, drop in 3 donuts at a time and cook until golden brown. Flip and allow the other side to become golden. Place on the cooling rack and repeat.

Glaze:

Mix all ingredients thoroughly and dip each donut into the glaze. Set on a rack to cool. Feel free to add other ingredients to make the glaze fun!

Carrot Cake

Often served at the Buen Provecho Restaurant

Ingredients:

1 cup sugar
¾ cup oil of choice
3 eggs
1½ cup flour

2 cups carrots
1 tsp baking soda
1½ tbsp cinnamon
1 tsp vanilla

Icing:

¼ cup cream cheese
1 cup icing sugar
1 tsp vanilla

1 drop of green food coloring
1 drop of orange food coloring

Directions:

Preheat the oven to 325°F and spray a rectangular baking pan with cooking spray.

Prepare carrots by peeling and grating them into a bowl and set aside. In a stand-up mixer combine eggs, vanilla, sugar, oil, and carrots. In another bowl, combine the remaining ingredients.

Combine wet and dry ingredients slowly. Stir until well combined and pour into a greased pan.

Bake at 325°F for one hour.

Remove it from the oven when you insert a toothpick into the center of the cake, and it comes out clean. Allow it to cool.

Icing:

In a stand-up mixer add 1 cup icing sugar and ¼ cup cream cheese and vanilla. Mix on high for 5 minutes. At first it will look very dry, but once it has been mixed on high for enough time it will be a smooth, creamy thick icing.

Place 3 tbsp of icing into each of two small bowls. To one bowl, add a drop of green food coloring and to the other bowl, add a drop of orange food coloring. Use the remaining white icing to cover the entire cake. Don't cut the cake into pieces.

Place green icing into a small sandwich bag and make a small slit in the corner of the bag. Repeat for the orange icing. You want to create little carrots on each piece. Start by making the carrot-like shape with the orange bag and then on top of the carrot add a dot of green icing for the carrot stem.

Serve and enjoy.

Susie

Hello, my name is Susana Cuevas. I feel blessed to be part of such a beautiful ministry as MNC. It is amazing to see how God changes lives in this place. My life was one of them. I was born in a traditional home to parents born in the state of Oaxaca. They raised me together with four other siblings. At the age of ten, I began to realize my parents had many problems. My father had a very strong character, and while they were still together, my mother had a relationship with another man. When my father found out, he began to hit her.

After many months, my mom decided to leave and left us alone with our father. This completely changed my life. I became the mother of my brothers, and it brought many responsibilities. My father became very controlling of me and at 13 I decided to leave my house to live with a boyfriend whom I had met only a month before.

Soon after moving in together, my partner started beating me. He used drugs and alcohol, and I started to drink alcohol because I believed if I drank, "I wouldn't feel the pain" when he hit me. My kidneys became sick due to the alcohol, to the point of urinating blood.

After a year of being with him, I decided to leave because he sent me to the hospital repeatedly and this made me very tired. I returned to live with my father, but I was very different, I was not happy. I related to drug addict friends, and I became addicted to crystal (meth). I was very vain and fake. Even when I was high, I tried drawing the attention of the men who sold me drugs. They gave me the drugs because of my beauty. I was a very promiscuous woman, having relationships with any man. I was surrounded all the time by drug-selling men, and I became very well known.

I started selling drugs to support my addiction. I consumed more and more and overdosed on two occasions. I remember fading away and foaming at the mouth. Twice I asked God for help and promised to change if He didn't let me die. But when I woke up, I just forgot my promises to God. My dad started going to church and when I went to visit my siblings, he hugged me and prayed for me.

I pushed him and cursed him. I had a lot of anger in my heart. At the time, I had a boyfriend whom I loved very much. When he discovered I was also seeing someone else, the relationship ended, and this plunged me deeper into drugs. I had a 40-year-old friend who was also a drug addict. She had a six-year-old daughter and on one occasion, I remember both of us, after using drugs, lying in bed with these men and looking over to see her six-year-old daughter sitting between the legs of one of these men. This terrified me because I knew there was a possibility my children would be sexually abused as I imagine the little girl probably was.

After years of consuming drugs, I began to have horrible nightmares. I would close my eyes and have terrible hallucinations and dreams to the point of not wanting to go to sleep. I began to use more and more drugs so I wouldn't sleep.

I had a third overdose and I begged God to help me. He met me in that moment, although I didn't know my life would be forever changed. After this experience, when I wanted to use drugs, I would just start crying and I couldn't figure out why. My friends made fun of me, so I went to another store to try and buy drugs made of other materials because I thought maybe the ingredients were the problem. However, every time I used drugs, I immediately started to cry. This got worse until one morning at dawn I started yelling at God, "I'm sick of this way of life! The only thing making me happy is drugs and now you're taking it away from me?"

I now see this was the power of God and the many prayers of my father. The next day, a 40-year-old woman who knew me told me she could help me. At the time, I was sleeping on the street and prostituting so I could do drugs and eat. My family was tired of me and refused to help me anymore. Now I see this as God closing that door of family help because it wasn't leading me get better, just helping me enough to get back on my feet then I would go back to the lifestyle I knew. This woman was the only one who was offering to help me. She took me to a men's rehabilitation center to ask if they could help me; they told me they would call me.

Incredibly, they called me in a week to tell me I would be the first resident of Peniel, the new women's rehabilitation center that was opening. The pastor of the center offered to pray for me for a full week. I spent one year in the rehabilitation center, and then my pastors, seeing my changed behavior and fear of God, asked me if I wanted to go to Bible school. There I met my husband and when we graduated, we decided to get married. We have been very blessed with two beautiful daughters. I am proud to be 20 years clean from drugs. We are teaching our daughters to love God and I am serving in my church. My chosen mother, Dorothy, has given me this opportunity to serve here at Mujeres Nuevo Comienzo. I am a living, breathing testimony of God changing lives. My dream is to die serving God because I owe everything to Him!!

Author's Note:

Susie started working at the mission in 2018. Serving others is her family's passion; her husband Sergio also serves at a neighboring mission. When I sat and talked with Susie, she shared she had met Dorothy 20 years prior, and she was the one who encouraged her to go to rehab. She believes the connection of her coming back to help others was orchestrated by God. She knows she is called to be part of the mission to help others find hope and life. Her family was blessed recently with a house build by a team of missionaries. When she is not helping on site at MNC, she bakes and decorates cakes as a side job.

She is a great example of what can happen if we choose to heal. When we allow God to bring joy and love to help us get out of the muck and mire of a trauma-filled life, we become more equipped to help others through their hurt. She carries hope and healing and demonstrates to the ladies and children how life can be better.

Creamy Chicken Dish

Susie's favorite dish to cook and share with her husband and two beautiful daughters.

Ingredients:

2 lbs. of chicken breasts
3 cloves of garlic
¼ onion
1 can of whole kernel corn

3 green pasilla chiles
2 cups sour cream
1 can of condensed chicken soup
2 tsp butter

Directions:

Preheat oven to 425°F. Place chiles in an oven-safe dish and place in oven for approximately 30 min. Turn them a few times while cooking. After removing them from the oven, place them in a plastic bag so the skins can sweat, making them easier to peel.

Cut the chicken breasts into cubes and fry in melted butter in a saucepan over medium heat.

Blend the garlic, onion, and a little water in the blender, and add the mixture to the cooked chicken breasts. Allow to simmer for.

Remove chilis from bag and peel by gently pulling at the blistered skin. The skins should come off easily to the touch. Remove all the seeds. Cut them into strips and add them into the saucepan with the chicken mixture. Then add the corn, sour cream, and can of condensed chicken soup. Stir together.

Enjoy over rice of choice and fresh bread!

See page 86 for Shabbat bread recipe.

Tres Leches Cake

Cake batter:

12 eggs
2 tsp baking powder
5 tbsp vanilla
1½ cups all-purpose flour

1½ cups pancake mix
1 cup sugar
½ cup milk

Tres leches milk mixture:

1 can condensed milk
1 can evaporated milk

1 cup milk

Directions:

Preheat the oven to 350°F and spray 2 round cake pans with cooking spray.

First, separate the yolks from the whites into a bowl. In a stand-up mixer, beat whites together until starting to get fluffy. Once they fluff, add sugar and continue to mix on high. Once they have tripled in volume, add the yolks and the vanilla. Continue to beat until the mixture is very fluffy and starting to have firm peaks. Turn the mixer down to a very slow speed. Add the milk and baking powder before adding the flour one tbsp at a time.

Pour batter into the prepared cake pans and place in the oven until you can insert a knife into the middle without it coming out with no batter on it, approximately 30 minutes.

Take the cake out to cool. Mix the three milks in a bowl and pour over the cake. Once milk has soaked into the cake, you can flip onto a flat tray and decorate if desired. If not, serve and enjoy!

Jorge

I am Jorge, the office manager for Mujeres Nuevo Comienzo. I came to serve at the mission in 2017. I met Dorothy at the church we were both attending several years ago. I was a Sunday school teacher there and worked as an engineer in the village. Many times, Dorothy would come to me and ask, "Jorge, can you help fix my computer?" I would help troubleshoot the problem she was experiencing and it was often the Wi-Fi needing to be reconfigured. One day, she called me and asked if I could help at MNC, and I have proudly been here ever since.

I agreed to serve at MNC enthusiastically. God gave me a heart for children! I want to help them grow with God and have good lives. There are many children who come longing for healing and hope with their mothers. It's so fulfilling to be part of the healing journey of those who come. It is incredible to watch them transform and gain a new outlook on life. Some have stayed in the community after leaving here and I still get to be a part of their lives, which brings me much joy. Outside the gates, former residents commonly tell me how grateful they are for the ministry and how their lives have changed.

A funny story I want to share is this: while Dorothy was baking one day, she heard the kids talking. They were chattering about who would take the ministry when Dorothy passed, and they said maybe Jorge! She shared the story with me, and it made me feel special. The kids see me as an important person in their lives, and I appreciate what God is doing for them.

We are very blessed to have many missionaries come volunteer here. All of their work is so important. There are many beautiful things to absorb here. When you look around, a painting on a wall isn't just a painting; it's a handprint on a ministry that is transforming lives. Not all who come here understand that; they just paint the wall and leave. My wish for those who come to serve is for them to intentionally see the women they are serving – truly see them and get to know them. Take a moment to understand their past and their current situation and get a picture of who they were and who they are now. It would help the residents see there are people who love them and are willing to help them, even though life has been ugly for them. Being seen and understood while being loved and valued is very important to help them acknowledge their own value.

I also want the women and children here to feel a sense of encouragement from others. For them to have hope and love helps them feel safe here. Those intentions pay off for years to come. They get excited to have visitors.

The ladies enjoy when others engage in prayer, play games or fútbol (soccer), and do activities with them and their children. They appreciate the people who come here to serve in whichever way they can.

In addition to volunteers from many countries, we have local supporters too. The board of directors helps guide and lead, and they donate time and resources here. Doctors from government services come every two weeks, dentists come when they are able, and local farmers will call and let us know when they have extra produce like zucchini, berries, tomatoes, or many other food blessings. These extra food donations are called 'gleanings' and are very important for our women to be able to cook their daily meals. It is encouraging to see them learn to cook healthy, nutritious meals for themselves and their children because of the generous donations.

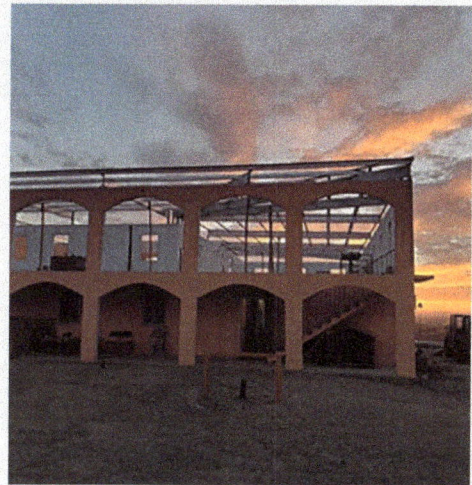

Every once in a while, other volunteers come. We have had artists and musicians who teach and encourage; churches that come to serve and hold Bible camps, and the local women's government section sends psychologists to give counsel and advice. Other counselors have come, as well. This past winter (2022), a hair salon came and set up on National Women's Day to bless the residents here.

God has bestowed many blessings at MNC. I have been very fortunate to observe many grandiose acts of God. The most incredible one I have witnessed here is the unbelievable way the roof was dreamed, created, and delivered.

Here is the story of the roof from an interview with Dorothy:

The main building was built in stages. As we received donations, we would build another portion. We broke ground in 2019 and it has been a work in progress ever since. God has had His hand in every detail. When it came time for the roof, many prayers were requested. The top floor had been finished and sealed several times, but water continued to leak down below and cause a lot of damage to the walls, the first-floor ceiling, and the floor.

Several groups come to MNC and tour while they are serving at other missions in the community. In one of the groups that came around that time, there was a man who recognized me from the time I had spent serving in the nuthouse (where macadamia nuts are processed) at the local orphanage. He was an engineer who had helped with a project for the nuthouse years prior. At first, he was in disbelief that the dream I had shared with him years ago about this ministry had come true and quite quickly. Visibly moved, he asked me what we needed. I knew exactly what his talent could bring, "A roof!"

The facility is nearly 10,000 square feet with a courtyard in the middle. No ordinary roof would be appropriate. We needed someone to create something special. He did just that: he designed an incredible roof leaving the center courtyard open, which is an art of engineering. A company in California fabricated the massive panels and when they were close to completion in the fall of 2021, we filed the paperwork to have the materials cross the border.

The shipment was scheduled to pass through the border in January of 2022 and was approved. The last week in December, we were notified of a change, and they would no longer allow the materials to come through without us paying taxes on it. The tax came to $11,000 U.S. dollars. The ministry did not have the money to pay, and as a Civil Association, this was previously approved tax-free. This left two loaded trucks sitting in Fresno waiting, and no gates would open.

We had to resubmit paperwork and in the middle of February, we received an appointment at the border. We were told there would be an open gate, and a team of us hustled to get there, arriving with five minutes to spare. The man conducting our interview was mean and sarcastic, scoffing at us for wanting everything for free and not supporting the country of Mexico.

I asked him, "Would you like to know what we do?" He angrily acquiesced and I told him about the purpose of the ministry, explaining that this shelter gives Mexican women a choice in life. It helps them be better citizens and mothers. Also, it provides support to them to get healthy, feel valuable, and build healthier communities, in turn building a healthier Mexico. "This is your future," I told him. He paused for a moment, then his tune changed rather quickly. Softly smiling he asked, "Would anyone like some coffee?"

So, the team and I sat and had coffee with him. A great friendship was formed with this unlikely encounter. This friendship paved the way for other Civil Associations to be able to bring in supplies to support their ministries as well. The roof came through and within weeks after the arrival, a volunteer crew arrived along with a few local helpers to install the massive blessing. God's timing is always the best timing.

This is yet another miraculous story of what presented as adversity turning into a blessing and proof of how God connects the dots. Another miracle concerns a lady who came to the mission a few years ago angry, confused, and full of hate. The gospel drastically changed Sara's life and transformed her to a woman full of love, compassion, and peace. She serves here now and is going to be the evening shift house mom on site. She is a great asset to the ministry.

I am truly grateful to be part of this ministry. It's always very busy, but I keep moving to make sure the reports and requests are filled and records are being kept, while still taking time for a game of fútbol with the kids. The blessings are physical too; every time I get injured or sick (like my wrist this week), it seems like being at the ministry brings quick healing. God is faithful to us.

The hardest part about working here is something that really tears my heart to pieces. It is when women come here hurt and destroyed and then leave the next day or a few days later because they choose not to accept the aid they need. Watching their children leave and miss out on the healing they could receive here... it's very hard to watch them walk away... it hurts my heart deeply. I know God has a plan and I must trust and believe He will be with them.

Thank you. I have so much gratitude for all the people who help this ministry. Thank you for reading this book and to all those who have come to serve here. Thank you to those who have toured MNC to learn more about what we do. Thank you to those who have been here and are part of the ministry and thank you to those who are going to come and serve. We appreciate you all greatly.

Author's Note:

Jorge is the only man featured in this book. Jorge and several men have been pillars of consistency and strength for MNC. He also received a house build in 2022. It is uncommon for men to receive one, but a team recognized the need to bless a deserving man who pours his heart into the ministry.

Emilia

My name is Emilia. I am 43 years old, and I have four beautiful daughters. I want to share my life before MNC. This story is about the lowest point in my life. Seven years ago, I was living in Ensenada with my boyfriend, who is also the father of three of my daughters. I was in the relationship for about 17 years, and we had lived together for nine years. On our third anniversary, we chose to celebrate trying drugs as a couple to have fun. This led to a very hard season of my life because something we started as a game turned out to be destructive. I had thought, "We have been together for three years, what could be wrong with doing drugs together?" What I didn't know was he had been using drugs previously. Drug use became a tornado in our life, consuming our relationship. He began openly and regularly indulging in drug use. He encouraged me to partake, and when I declined to join him, he resorted to violence, commanding me to use against my will.

When I was pregnant with our last baby Ana, things were supposed to change, but they didn't. My boyfriend became more aggressive to the point where the physical abuse was seen in public. I was so humiliated; the continued display of abuse grew until I thought I could no longer endure it.

At six months pregnant, I thought my only options were to put the baby up for adoption or terminate the pregnancy. When I shared this with him, all he said was, "Terminating the pregnancy is good with me and if you want to put her up for adoption, look for rich people to pay good money for her." Sadly, I realized there was nothing I could do to satisfy him; only money could. I searched for adoption options on the internet, but my efforts were unsuccessful. As I sat confused and alone, I turned the idea over and over in my mind whether or not to terminate the pregnancy. Finally, I came to my senses, and I decided I did have the ability and strength to raise my children by myself. I also realized I didn't need him to survive, and in order to survive I had to leave, but wasn't ready yet.

Two weeks before I delivered the baby, he beat me very badly in the stomach. He said, "If you don't want to have her then I am going to help you lose her!" But the real reason he wanted the baby gone was because I refused to make money by sleeping with other men. He was insistent I needed to do so, and I told him no. When the beating did not change my mind, he threatened to kick me and our daughters out. So, I left with our daughters, and we slept in the streets for the night. The next day, I took the girls to my husband's mother because I was desperate, and we needed a place to stay. Soon after, I decided to go back and he beat me again, although he will say he never remembers beating me.

I was not working, and my boyfriend refused to work, so my oldest daughter, at age 14, was the only one working and supporting our home.

When Ana came, I had her in the hospital and her dad refused to go. When I returned home from the hospital and showed him his new baby girl, his response was, "She's pretty but do you have any money?" I said, "I don't have any money, I was in the hospital delivering your baby!" It was evident to me that if I didn't have money, he didn't care about us. I decided to leave him again.

Once I had a home and a job, he reappeared in our existence, coming and going from my home when I was at work. A sense of unease grew in my stomach, and before long, I unraveled the truth: he was prostituting himself with other men. I informed him that he was no longer welcome in my space, yet no one could successfully remove him from my home.

I was so exhausted and defeated. I was working the night shift, would come home in the morning, cook and clean, and go to the next job. I was so down and hopeless and planned to run away. Out of desperation, I wrote a letter to my daughters to say goodbye.

Ana was only five months old. I was overwhelmed and our circumstances were so daunting. Two days after I wrote the letter, I realized if I left, I would not only be leaving my daughters; I would be leaving them in the same hole I was in. I was angry with God. I yelled at Him, "Where are you?" and I heard a voice that said, "I am here. Look here," and I saw Ana sleeping in the bed. This gave me strength and I told myself to be strong for her and get out of there. I felt so low, I just cried and cried but I was eventually able to gain enough strength to move forward.

A few days later, I burned the letter I had written to my girls and went to the house of my ex-boyfriend's mother. My youngest sister, whom I love very much, was there and she told me, "You should see yourself. You are dying of drugs. I will give you one hour to make a decision, or I am going to call social services."

I knew I couldn't do this alone; the burden on my shoulders was just too big to carry anymore. She was right – this needed to stop. I went back to our place and my ex was there eating my food and demanding more. He was angry with me for not making him breakfast. I went to the room and grabbed all of my daughters' papers, a change of clothes, and my girls. As I was leaving, my ex commanded me to bring him more food. On my way out the door, I turned to him and said, "I hope one day you can figure out you lost your family." I left with my three youngest girls. Caris, my oldest, did not want to come. She was in disbelief that I would follow through and exhausted by my past promises to change.

As I was walking up a hill on my journey, I looked to God and said, "You helped me get out; show me where to go." I found a police station where we went inside, and they said they could look for a place where someone could help us. I had to give a report and when I was done, they said they could find a place to help. The police asked about contacting one of my family members, but I refused. I did not want anyone to know where I was. After so many years of suffering, I wanted to be left alone.

I was living in Ensenada, and they called many places, but they couldn't find room for us. The officer came back after 15 minutes and said he found one place quite far away in the desert of San Quintin valley. I wanted to go. On the drive there, I had so much peace and felt like God was embracing me and saying, "I am here. Everything is going to be okay." Going to MNC as I learned to let go and trust God has been the best decision of my life. I am so grateful for this place (MNC).

Author's Note:

Emilia stayed at MNC and was able to get drug-free and make a new life for herself and her daughters. She learned to be a chef and was working in the kitchen at the Buen Provecho (the restaurant at MNC). She saved the money to buy a piece of land, was accepted to the list to have a house built, and a ministry built a home for herself and her girls.

She is still doing well and is taking great care of her life.

Azteca Soup

Ingredients:

2 lbs of corn tortillas, page 74
4 tomatoes
½ onion
¼ cup cotija cheese (queso fresco)
¼ cup sour cream
1 avocado

1 oregano leaf
1 chicken bouillon cube
½ cup oil of choice
4 cups water
2 garlic cloves

Directions:

Cut the tortillas into strips. Heat the saucepan on high heat and add 1 tsp of oil. Fry tortilla strips and set aside.

Press garlic and chop onion and tomatoes. Heat saucepan with 1 tablespoon oil on medium heat. Add garlic, onions, and tomatoes. Once a paste is starting to form, add 4 cups of water, chicken bouillon cube, and oregano.

Let boil. Place tortillas into a bowl and pour soup on top. Top with avocado, sour cream, and cheese.

Luna

My name is Luna, and I am a single mother of four daughters. I am from the State of Chiapas (Tapachula). I arrived at Mujeres Nuevo Comienzo on June 16, 2022.Although my process did not start here, this circle is part of God the Creator's plan for my life. When I came here, there were so many people I didn't know. I was invaded by anxiety when each look fell on me. Inside, I held so much hatred and resentment for the life imposed on me. I blamed every person for what I was going through. I wanted to destroy these people.

I tried to keep to myself as much as possible. One day, another mom called me over in private and wanted to know more about me. Everything I was trying to hold in came out in tears. I felt so miserable because my past has so much sadness and pain. Even so, I was able to answer her and then I pleaded, asking that nobody take my daughters away from me. They were my only reasons to fight. I cried even more as this person hugged me because in that moment, she was everything I always wished my mother would be for me.

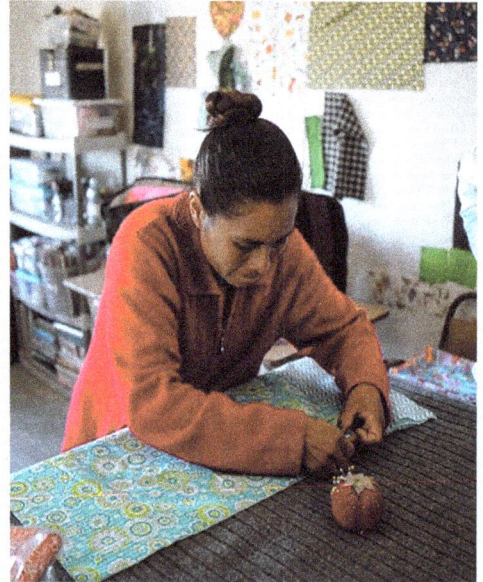

Both my mother and siblings thought I was rubbish. They believed I was so insignificant and worthless. When I was younger, a little white spot formed in my eye. It kept spreading, so we went to see a doctor. He said I had a disease there was no treatment for, and I would never see again from my right eye. Because of this, many family members and friends believed I would end up being a beggar on the streets.

At MNC, I was cared for, loved, and protected. I never knew a feeling of belonging before. I have learned to carry the Bible, the Word of God with me. Before coming to this ministry, I only read the Bible when my strength was running out. It was like recharging myself. Here at MNC, we read the Bible and pray every morning. Reading and praying have helped me to be able to cross every obstacle that arises during each day. I do not deny I still get angry, but no longer to the degree of wanting to destroy everything. The women and I do so many things together, and I love their company more and more. One thing I am still learning is to demonstrate the love of God. This is still hard for me. The most important thing of all has been accepting myself as I am and beginning to love others.

> *"Keep this Book of the Law always on your lips; meditate on it day and night, so that you may be careful to do everything written in it. Then you will be prosperous and successful." Joshua 1:8 (NIV)*
> *"For he will command his angels concerning you to guard you in all your ways". Psalm 91:11 (NIV)*

Author's Note:

Luna lived at MNC for nine months and then in transition housing for six months. She currently works at a local mission and plans to open a restaurant someday.

Barbacoa

Ingredients:

2 pounds beef roast
1 tbsp vinegar
1 tbsp soy sauce
3 mulato chilies
3 cascabel chilies
3 pasilla chilies

1 tbsp cinnamon
1 tsp black pepper
1 onion, chopped
1 tbsp oil
Garlic to taste
Cloves and cumin to taste

Directions:

Marinate the roast with vinegar and soy sauce for at least one hour in the refrigerator. Heat frying pan over medium heat with 1 tablespoon oil, add remaining ingredients, and cook until onion is translucent.

Move ingredients from frying pan to blender, blend until smooth to create the sauce. Put the roast into a large baking dish and add the sauce from the blender. Cover baking dish, place in oven at 325°F, and cook for 5 hours or until the meat is soft and tender. Shred the beef. Add salt to taste.

Olivia

My name is Olivia, and I was born in 1988 in the state of Veracruz. I am the youngest of my parents' children. My childhood had many sad moments including my father dying of cancer when I was only four years old. My mother and I formed a special bond as we mourned his loss.

At the age of nineteen, I met a man who became my partner and during our relationship, we had two sons. The statement "love is blind" is true. In the beginning, I did not know that drinking could be so damaging to our relationship. I felt very confused and hopeless for most of our time together. His drinking increased and towards the end, we tried several things to fix what was broken.

At one point, we went to live in San Quintin in search of a better future. However, it didn't help and only encouraged his drinking to increase even more. I knew I needed to separate from him to stay safe. So, I took the boys and left to find a better, safer, happier life for us.

While we were in San Quintin, my mother passed away. I was devastated. She was my rock and my support; she meant everything to me. I was crushed and lost without her, but I had to keep going, trying to provide a life for my boys.

A little while later, I started a relationship with another man. We had a little girl together. It was very difficult living with him. He rejected my sons and made life very difficult for us. The neglect turned into violence, and I no longer wanted to be with him. The violence became threats to hurt my children, myself, and my family. To punish me, he would take away my daughter and wouldn't return her for days. It was such a terrifying time. I felt helpless and defeated. I didn't have anyone to help me, and I didn't have anywhere to go. I was desperate for a different life. I gathered the strength to leave. I left everything except my children, and we went to a ministry I heard about that could help us.

MNC supported me in everything I needed physically and emotionally. Our lives changed dramatically. The most important thing I learned here is the Word of God. Abuela and the volunteers here have shown me the immense love God has for us. Now I feel calm, valuable, and at peace. I am very grateful to God for the people who make this place possible.

After one and a half years of being a part of this ministry, God gave me the opportunity to have a home built for my family. Now, I have a safe home for my children who are 12, ten, and four years old. I want a better future for us. I already got baptized and I want to stand firm in this journey of faith in God and teach my children to be His servants also. Now my children and I know we have a heavenly Father who protects us, who will never leave us. I have faith knowing God provides for us all our needs and I want to serve Him with all my heart.

I am working towards starting my own business so I can be home and have more time for my children and for God. I put all my trust in God for each day and to guide our lives.

Tamales Veracruzanos

For the Tamales:

2 cups of corn flour
½ cup lard or butter
2½ cups pork broth
1 tsp salt

½ cup milk
10 banana leaves
¼ tsp baking powder

For the Relleno:

1 pound cooked and shredded pork tenderloin

For the Mole:

4 guajillo chiles
1 pasilla chile
2 ancho chiles
2 cloves of garlic
1 banana
1 cinnamon stick
50g (2oz.) toasted sesame seeds
50g (2oz.) raisin
50g (2oz.) dried pumpkin seeds

2 ground Ritz crackers
¼ dark chocolate bar
¼ cup oil of choice
2 roasted red tomatoes
½ onion
¼ tsp cumin
½ tsp pepper
1 tsp salt
1 tbsp oil

Directions:

First, place the pork tenderloin in a large pot with 2 cups of water and 1 tsp salt. Boil on medium/high heat until the roast is cooked through the middle or at 165°F in the middle. Cut pork into roughly 2-inch by 2-inch cubes.

The Tamale Dough:

Mix the dry ingredients (corn flour, baking powder, and salt). Next, add the lard and milk. Next, add the broth from the tenderloin until you get a dough with a soft liquid consistency. Let it rest while you prepare the mole.

The Mole:

Heat a medium size frying pan on medium heat. Place all the chiles in the pan with 1 tablespoon oil and fry until they are browned. Add pressed garlic, chopped onion, and remaining ingredients and fry them well. Add the ingredients from the frying pan into the blender. Blend until you have a smooth sauce, approximately 1.5 minutes. Pour the sauce back into the pan and add the pork tenderloin cubes to marinate while you prepare the tamales. Turn to low heat and allow to simmer.

Place the banana leaf on a hot griddle for two minutes on the first side and flip for one more minute on the next side. Cut the banana leaves into 12-inch squares. On a plate lay the banana leaf flat and spread a layer of tamale dough ¼ inch thick. Add 1 tbsp mole sauce and pork tenderloin on top of the maseca dough. Fold the leaf carefully into a rectangle, ensuring all the ingredients are secured in the leaf. Place into a large soup pot. Repeat until you use all your ingredients. Add enough water to cover two inches of the bottom of the pot. Seal the pot well with a lid and place it on the stove. Cook on medium/high for one hour.

Ava

I have three children, ages 14, eight, and six years old, and we arrived at the ministry on April 20, 2022. My husband at the time, the father of my children, was very violent when he was using drugs. In the beginning of our relationship, he was kind and decent, but when he used drugs, he turned very violent and mean. Early in our marriage, he and I started going to church, he accepted Jesus. When I saw he was changing, I remember being so happy. I also accepted Jesus as my Lord and my Savior and then we were baptized. We continued going to church for a time, but eventually went less and less until we stopped altogether.

After we stopped going, he went back to drugs. He became more aggressive than before, jealous, and arrogant when he was under the influence of drugs. This caused many arguments and fights. Sometimes he would stop for a short time when he realized what he was doing. Then he would start again. Our lives were a continuous cycle of happiness and then abuse from 2011 until April 19th of 2022. His aggression grew more intense, and he would hit me. During the night, he wouldn't let me sleep because when he was drugged, he wanted to have sex all the time. I told him not to bother me and out of exasperation told him I would not have sex with him while he was using. He started to insult me and accuse me of being pregnant. I insisted I was not pregnant, and he took out his belt and hit me twice with it. My daughter and mother-in-law intervened and told him he needed to calm down. Many times, I cried out to God begging, "Why, my Lord? How long do I have to live like this?" I finally told Him (God) I couldn't live like that anymore.

The next day, my husband went to work, but he came home around noon and I was taking a bath. He started accusing me of sleeping with another man because I was bathing. I explained to him that living like this was very difficult and I couldn't keep doing it. I told him I was going to report him to the police station, and he told me, "Let's go at once, because you don't know what I'm capable of." When we arrived at the station, they took my statement and arrested him immediately.

The "purple squad" (police who help women in abusive situations) took me and asked if I wanted to go to a shelter. I was apprehensive but my sister-in-law who accompanied me told me it was for the best, so I reluctantly accepted. I thank God for bringing me to this place. He listened to my prayers in my moments of anguish. Thank God for the life of Abuela, Sister Susie, Vicky, and Brother Jorge. Thank God for all the people who donate money and food and help the MNC women's ministry.

God bless all the people who work and help this ministry.

Author's Note:

Ava lived at MNC for eight months and then moved to transition housing for seven months. She recently married and is doing well in life.

Chiles Rellenos with Cheese and Tomato Salsa

Ingredients:

6 Poblano peppers
1½ cups grated cheese
2 tbsp sour cream
5 eggs

3 tbsp flour
2 cups oil of choice
(chicken, beef, or shrimp is optional)

Ingredients for the Red Salsa:

4 medium red tomatoes
2 Serrano peppers
½ onion

one clove of garlic
one chicken broth cube
1 cup water

Directions:

First, heat a frying pan and roast the chiles in the pan until all sides darken in color.

When the peppers are well roasted, place them in a bag for about 5 minutes to loosen the skin. Remove the skin and all the seeds. Grate the cheese and stuff the chiles with the cheese. Use toothpicks to close the peppers so the cheese doesn't come out.

OPTIONAL: Add desired meat into the chiles.

Beat the eggs and submerge each stuffed chile in the beaten egg mixture. Heat 2 cups of oil in a frying pan. Sprinkle the chiles with a little flour and fry them in the hot oil until the coating is crispy. In a saucepan, boil the tomatoes and serrano peppers in one cup of water.

After boiling, pour the mixture into a blender and add the onion, garlic, and chicken broth cube. Once it is smooth, pour the sauce into the frying pan with the chiles for a few minutes.

Serve the chile relleno on a plate with sour cream on top.

Marta

I was born in Baja California, and I have a very beautiful and intelligent daughter. Life growing up was a bit difficult. My parents separated when I was eight years old, and my mother had another partner. My little brother and I lived with my mother and two of my brothers lived with my father. My mom worked a lot and I almost never saw her. I lived many years sad and alone.

When I was 14, I met my daughter's father. At first, he was my friend. As we spent more time together, he became my boyfriend. We broke up because I didn't feel good about him using drugs. Two years later, I went back to him. We were together for more than a year when I got pregnant. When he drank, he would hit me. He made accusations of the baby not being his, and after our baby was born, he became increasingly violent. I don't know what snapped in his head. I remember being inside the room with the baby with the door closed. He began to hit the door, but I would not open it. Thankfully, he wasn't able to hurt me that day in his rage because my brother-in-law arrived and helped me get out of the room. My boyfriend left the house and the next day he came back all calm and back to normal.

I tried to make him happy and take care of the home. I would cook our meals but if he didn't like what I made, he would go eat with his mom and leave me by myself. I ate by myself often. When our daughter and I went to visit my mother, he would get upset but he didn't want to accompany me. The relationship felt very one-sided.

One day, out of the blue, he began to beat me in the head with the remote control for the TV. Afterward, he kicked me out of the house. I went to stay with my mom. Eventually, he felt remorseful and came to ask me to go back to our home. The abuse did not stop though, and I don't know why I stayed to endure it. He would hit, kick, beat me with a belt, and scratch my face. Once, he even tried to suffocate me with a blanket, but I somehow had the strength to take it off.

Along with the physical abuse, he would verbally assault me. He would tell me I was worthless because I had endured sexual violence. He treated me like trash. He would slander me, saying I was a prostitute and that I had cheated on him. Many times, I separated from him, but I always went back. He worked and made good money, but would barely give me enough to buy food. My mother-in-law supported me; she helped me when I had no food. My mom and dad also helped when they saw I was struggling. I never said anything to my family because I was so ashamed.

We lived together for almost 11 years, and the last year was the most difficult. The violence escalated to him using a knife to assault me. He yelled at me constantly, and I lived in fear of what would happen if I didn't appease him. My daughter didn't want to live with us because I was so stressed, I would scream at her too. One day during a fight, my daughter went to my mother and told her about the abuse. She hurriedly told my father. My father came immediately and called the police. The police arrived, and I was able to take a few of my belongings but my abuser hid. My father told me about a shelter, and I agreed to go there for my daughter's sake. On the way to the shelter, as I stared out the window of the police truck, I saw some white butterflies and they brought peace to my heart.

To this day I have not gone back. We go to church now and have a lot of peace in our lives. God met me where I was. I am learning to be stronger and have better self-esteem. I have also learned to sew, make bread, and bake cookies. Abuela (Dorothy) has taught me many other things. My daughter and I are happy here too.

At MNC I see a lot of butterflies, an assurance of peace in my life. I am very grateful to God and to Abuela for giving me a new life. I am happy and grateful to the people who serve here. Thank you for everything.

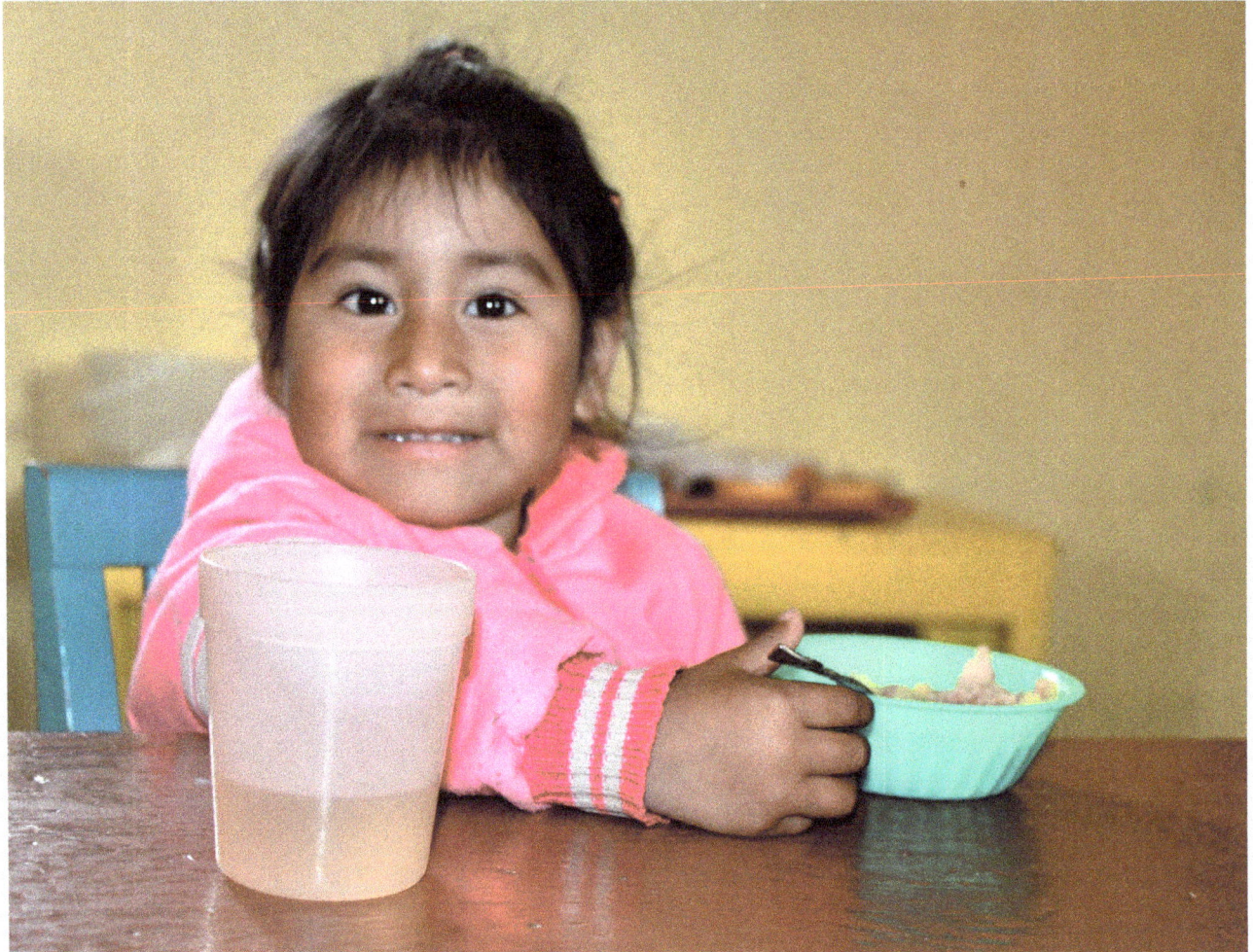

Garlic Rice

Ingredients:

2 cups cooked rice
½ onion
4 cloves of garlic
2 chicken broth cubes

4 cups chicken broth
¼ cup butter
1 can of sweet corn

Directions:

In a large frying pan, melt butter on medium heat. Place rice into the frying pan and allow it to brown.

While the rice is browning, boil onion and garlic in a small pot of water with the chicken broth cubes.

Once water has been boiling for about 3 minutes, remove onion and garlic and blend until smooth. Add onion, garlic, browned rice, corn, and chicken broth into a pot. Place a lid on top and allow it to boil. Allow to simmer for about 10 minutes or until the water is absorbed.

Sofia

"Do not be anxious about anything, but in every situation, by prayer and petition, with thanksgiving, present your requests to God. And the peace of God, which transcends all understanding, will guard your hearts and your minds in Christ Jesus." Philippians 4:6-7 (NIV)

"… In you, Lord my God, I put my trust." Psalm 25:1 (NIV)

"Trust in the LORD with all your heart And do not lean on your own understanding. In all your ways acknowledge Him, And He will make your paths straight." Proverbs 3:5-7 (NKJV)

These verses gave me strength in hard times.

Hello. My name is Sofia, and I am 23 years old. I have a son and two daughters. I grew up working on a vegetable farm in Acapulco, Mexico; raised by my grandma and aunts. My mom was 15 when I was born, and she left me with my grandmother after she had me. I never knew my father. My grandmother raised me along with many of my cousins, who were like siblings to me. We were close and did normal family things like chores and cooking food together. My grandmother taught me how to read and write, but I never went to school.

When I was 10 years old, my grandmother passed away from cancer. It was like a bomb went off for us; there was immense loss and darkness. My life felt like it ended that day, I was lost and scattered. After she passed, my cousins and I were all separated, as we no longer had a home. I was required to go live with strangers: my mom, her boyfriend, and my other siblings. The first time meeting my mother was uncomfortable. She didn't know me, and I quickly realized from her cold and mean behavior she didn't want to know me. I had so many emotions: uncertainty, apprehension, and anxiety. I had no choice in the matter.

My mom had five other children and I became her slave. While she was working in the camps (field labor), I would have to do all the laundry, cook all the food, clean, and watch all the kids. One night when I was 11, her boyfriend touched my body and sexually assaulted me. I screamed and cried out. He lied and convinced my mom I was crazy, and nothing had happened. She accused me of lying and kicked me out of the house for causing trouble.

I went to live with my grandfather's girlfriend. Living there was not working well, so I had to go back to my mother's. When I was 12 years old, her boyfriend started giving me crystal drugs (meth). I don't remember what happened when I used, but I found it numbed my pain. A few years later, at 14, my mom told me I was going to work in a store. She sent me to live with a lady I had never met. Upon arrival, I realized the "store" was a bar. My job was not to serve beer or food but to satisfy the men who bought me however they wished. My mom sold me into prostitution, and I was unable to escape.

After a year, my mom sent for me, and soon after, we ended up at a women's shelter (MNC). She had decided to leave her boyfriend because there was so much violence and abuse and there was no money to support everyone. We were there for six months until my uncle sent money for us to move to Mexico City with him. I was told to stay home again while my mom worked to take care of all the children and housework. I still did not go to school.

One day, the father of my siblings — my mom's abuser and the man who sexually abused me — reached out to my mom. She refused to answer for a while but eventually answered the phone and he begged for her to come home. She was considering whether or not to go and asked me if he had actually tried to touch me. I lied and told her no because I wanted her to go back to the bad man and experience pain — deep pain — like I had been forced to. I was filled with so much hatred for my mother and wanted her to hurt as much as I hurt because of her choices. We returned to live with him. Sadly, I was also willing to live in pain just for her to live in it.

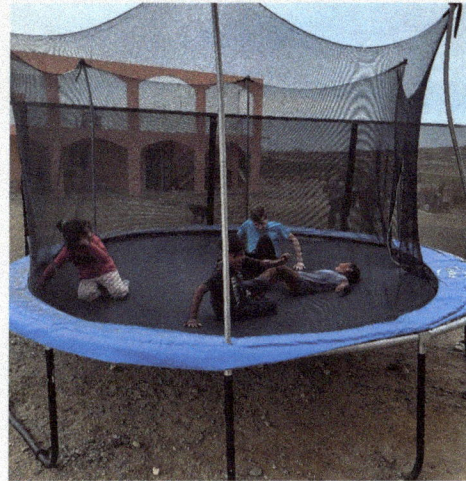

When I was 16, I started working in the fields. I met a man there who was selling bread. He was a married man, but I became his girlfriend. I liked the attention he gave me, and he was very kind to me. I hadn't felt kindness since my grandmother passed away. We would sneak out during the nights, but I still lived with my family. Early in our relationship, I got pregnant. I told him about the pregnancy, but he didn't believe the baby was his.

When my mom found out I was pregnant, she accused me of sleeping with my stepdad. They rejected me and didn't want me living with them, but I had nowhere to go. I came and left a few times as they would have pity for a day or two and then kick me back out. One day, I met a lady who knew of a woman named Dorothy. She said Dorothy had a shelter called Mujeres Nuevo Comienzo. I remembered her from when I was 14 and we stayed a short time. The lady told me when I was ready, I should call her and she would come get me. I ended up calling her, but the decision was very difficult. I was the one who bathed all my siblings, fed them, did their laundry, and took care of them all the time. The children cried and begged me not to leave them. Even though it was so hard, I did end up calling this woman to come get me.

I came to MNC with so much hate and anger. I had lived so many years confused. I'd had such a good life with my grandmother and then I was catapulted into a torrential life of being used and treated worse than the dogs in the street. At MNC, I started to hear about a God who loves me, sees me, and created me beautifully. Little by little, my heart started to change. My baby boy helped me get the courage to change and I desired to give him a better future and life. I often would want to leave the women's shelter, but I had to really remember what kind of life I wanted to give my son.

This ministry helped me change – change the way I think and how I lived. I learned how to cook, parent, and love, and now I have two beautiful daughters and a husband. I get to work at the training center restaurant and my children go to school and are in the daycare here.

Author's Note:

Sofia works at Buen Provecho as a waitress. She appreciates that her children can stay at the guardería (childcare center) while she works. She is married and is doing well in her heart.

Lia

I grew up far from town in the mountains of Oaxaca, Mexico with my family, who were shepherds. We did not have a house to live in, so we slept under rocks or whatever makeshift shelter we could erect. We would build fires at night to stay warm and if the fire went out because of the rain, we would have no heat and no fire to cook on. My father suffered from mental health issues, which caused my mother to cry a lot since it was difficult for her to see my father so unwell.

Due to the difficulty of living, my parents took me to an orphanage at age six so I could go to school. They would come to visit me every six months. Now I think it was good for me, but as a six-year-old, it was very difficult to be away from my family. When I was eight, I moved back home to the mountains with my family. I remember a long day riding our horse to town because we needed to get supplies. Due to my dad's many mental illnesses, he forgot I was with him and rode away too fast. I ran after him, but eventually he was out of sight. I was lost and it took me a whole day to find a house where I could get help. I was so scared, but a kind family helped me find my family.

When I was 10, there was a huge storm and my mom and dad left to find new pastures. I was left alone with my older brothers and two younger siblings who were five and two. The storm wiped out what shelter we had built, and many of our animals died. I believed my siblings and I were going to die there alone. I was afraid and unsure of what to do. My parents continued to move around looking for new pastures for the sheep. We still did not travel with them, we stayed, waiting together.

While they were gone, one of my older brothers started emotionally, physically, and sexually abusing me. He told me, "You are good for nothing." I did not tell my mom about what he would do to me for three years. Eventually, I refused to go tend the sheep with him because he would hurt me there. She would be upset with me for refusing to go. I was angry and hurt. My mom and I started to fight and yell because she didn't understand why I was starting to be so defiant.

When I was 13, my mom got sick with cancer, and she left us to live in the hospital for two years. I had to stay behind and take care of my two younger siblings. When my mom returned, my family was scattered. I moved in with my other older brother and his wife to take care of their cows. While I was living with them, a lady who knew me asked me why I was still living in the middle of nowhere where it was so dangerous and where there is no civilization. She invited me to go to Chihuahua to live and work with her there. I accepted and left without telling my parents. After six months, I was able to return and bring some money back with me.

Flour Tortillas

Ingredients:

2 cups flour
⅔ cup of water

2 tbsp oil of choice

Directions:

Place all ingredients in a large bowl. Knead for 10 minutes. Cover the bowl with a cloth and let the dough rest for 10 minutes. Roll the dough into desired size for your tortillas. Press the balls very thin and flat using a tortilla press or pie pan. Heat a saucepan or griddle to medium-high heat and fry the tortilla for 15 seconds or until you see it bubbling and getting brown spots. Flip tortilla and cook for 30 more seconds. Lastly, flip once again and cook for 15 more seconds. Your tortilla should be bubbling and soft with a golden color. You will notice your tortillas getting hard if you are overcooking them.

Chilaquiles

Ingredients:

3 cups oil of choice for frying tortillas
2 lbs of corn tortillas, page 74
Monterey jack cheese
½ cup tomato puree
5 red tomatoes

½ onion
3 green chiles
one bundle of cilantro
½ cup water
Salt to taste

Directions:

First, take your corn tortillas and cut them into quarters. You will have four triangles. Continue until you have cut all your tortillas into quarters. Heat three cups of oil in a frying pan and add a handful of tortillas at a time. Cook until golden and remove from oil. Repeat until all the tortillas are fried.

In a frying pan, add a tsp of oil. Chop tomatoes, onion, cilantro, and chiles. Fry the tomatoes, onions and chiles until brown. Once fried, add the tomato puree, ½ cup water, and cilantro. Allow to boil. Then add the crispy tortilla chips and top with as much cheese as you like. Once cheese is melted, serve.

Sara

I grew up in Oaxaca working at the markets selling food with my mother and grandmother. When I was barely 15, I met a man who was eight years older than me. I soon became pregnant and had my first child before turning sixteen. Not feeling confident I could take care of my son; I left him with my parents and went to the U.S. to work. My mom was worried for my safety and made me travel with a man I did not like. I protested but she was insistent. While working in the States, I became pregnant again. The father of the baby lost his business, and we separated, so I made my way back to Oaxaca. Shortly after having my second son, I became deeply depressed and started drinking heavily. How could I keep making such poor decisions? Life was not going well. When my oldest son turned thirteen, I decided to go back to the States to work. My two sons stayed with my parents.

While in the States, I fell in love with a man. He drank but I accepted the behavior because I loved him so much. Together we had two children, a boy and a girl. I slowly began drinking with him, which led to me drinking more and more. The alcohol led to many problems in our relationship. We began fighting nonstop.

One time, my dad called and asked me to come back home. He promised me a job at a family business if I came. I decided to go back home, taking my two young children with me. When I arrived, the plans did not work out for the job, and I was left to figure it out on my own. I was really struggling, and life was tough. I was trying to provide for my children and pay for childcare. The stress was hard for me, so I did what I knew, and began drinking again.

A friend of mine came to me and said she had a place where I could make money and drink at the same time. It sounded enticing, so I decided to try it out. When I arrived for the first day, I discovered it was a nightclub. I chose to stay and work there. The job was wild; I partied a lot with my coworkers and the patrons. It didn't take long until I was consuming drugs too.

It wasn't a safe job to work at; the lifestyle invited a lot of bad behavior. One night, I remember leaving and some men tried to push me to their truck. They were sex traffickers trying to abduct me. I ran and ran and hid in the woods. I stayed there as long as I could. A car pulled up at some point and I thought they had found me, but it was someone there to help. I continued working there so I could pay my bills, but eventually friends and co-workers started giving me money and told me to go make a better life for myself.

I then decided I needed to go back to the U.S., yet again leaving my children behind. This time, I got stuck in Mexicali and wasn't able to cross the border. My sister called me and told me my youngest son had broken his arm and needed a specialist. I went back to get him and take my two younger children with me to Mexicali.

The specialist said my son needed an expensive surgery, but I could not afford it, so we put him in a cast instead. Twenty days later, my daughter fell and hit her head. She was only five years old. Her eyes turned white, and I was so scared she would die. The doctor said there was not much they could do besides give her an injection for pain. As the doctor was preparing to give her the injection, she woke up and hollered, "No shots!" The doctor was very surprised. They gave her a neck brace to help her, and we were able to leave the hospital.

We had to go in for check-ups and I had to go to the clinic with my four-year-old son in a cast and my five-year-old daughter in a neck brace. People were very judgmental and treated me as an abusive mother. The pressure was stressful, and I drank to cope. I left Mexicali and went to Trinidad because the weather was better, and I wanted to get away from the judgmental people. There I got into a bad relationship. It was toxic and abusive. It was so bad, my brother came and took my children back to Oaxaca with him. I tried hard to get away from the relationship but kept failing. I ended up praying to a God I didn't know. Somehow, all the doors opened. I was able to escape the relationship and make it to Ensenada.

I decided I wanted my children back, so I went home to Oaxaca. My parents would not give them to me if I was still using, so I lied and told them I was sober and was going to be a good mom to them. Of course, I was still using drugs to continue coping. When my parents discovered I had lied, they threatened to call DIF (the National System for Integral Family Development). Fearing I would lose them again, I chose to go to a ministry I heard about when I was in Trinidad – a place called Mujeres Nuevo Comienzo in Vicente Guerrero.

I didn't have the money to get to the ministry, so we had to hide from my parents for three days while I searched for a ride. I found a ride in the back of a truck and went as far as I could. We were in the truck for several days. When I made it close to Vicente Guerrero, I tried to call a cousin in the area to finish helping me get there. I could not reach her, but I met a woman who took us the rest of the way. I was full of insecurity wondering if they would have room or if they'd let me stay. When I arrived, I was well received by Susie.

I came from an idolatrous family who worshiped saints. I didn't tell anyone at the ministry but just hid them. Susie gave me my first Bible; it was different and refreshing. Before coming to MNC I had never read a Bible. She led devotionals every morning and one day she explained what idols were and it confused me. I asked God to show me if it was wrong to pray to these idols whom I have worshiped all my life. While I was looking for my idol, God showed me something from what I had learned in devotionals earlier in the morning. The devotional talked about David and Goliath and how he slayed his giant by striking him in the head because God directed him to. God showed me right then I needed to take my idols to the garbage bin.

I lived in a trailer at the mission with my daughter and son. Little by little, I learned about God, and it transformed my life. My kids were happy and didn't want to leave. I started to see a difference in myself as I was getting to know God too. Over time, I was liberated from addiction and evil. Susie said one time when she prayed for me, she was aware that something evil left. It was a new experience for her and me.

God started putting things back in order in my life. I reached out to the father of my children born in the U.S. and he agreed to pay child support. I was able to find forgiveness and receive forgiveness from my mom and my children for my past actions and poor choices. After a year at MNC, I decided I wanted to go back to the U.S. Dorothy helped me make the appointments with the Visa office. My younger son got sick, and I missed the appointment because I was taking care of him. Asher (a local missionary at YWAM) told me to pray about the paperwork. There were people ready to build my family a house, but it would depend on whether I chose to use the money to go back to the States or use it to finish buying my property so they could build a house. The clear answer from God was to stay, buy the property, and to get a house instead of going back to the U.S.

During the height of the COVID pandemic, my oldest son got really sick. He needed oxygen, and the doctors thought he was going to die. Through all of it, Dorothy was so encouraging, and the ministry helped financially when I was in great need regarding my son. It was a challenging time and Abuela and the mission helped me to keep going.

Before I came to MNC I wasn't a good person. For some reason God chose to protect me through drug use, alcohol abuse, and an attempted trafficking abduction. I sought the Lord with all my heart, and He forgave me all my sins. He did a miracle in me, and I had an encounter with Him.

I am very grateful for this place. I have a whole new life. I don't know where I would be without this place. I wish there were more ministries like it here. Please pray for more people to want to do what Dorothy is doing; women in Mexicali and Oaxaca need help too. More women like me need help and we need more places like this in the world. I now worship Jesus and I continue to pray for my family who don't know our Father God. God is here and God is real.

> *For God so loved the world that he gave his only begotten Son, so that everyone who believes in him may not perish but have eternal life. For God did not send his son into the world to condemn the world, but that the world might be saved through him.*

John 3:16-17 (NAB)

Sopes o Gorditas

Ingredients:

1 cup maseca (corn flour)
Approximately 1 liter of water
½ cup refried beans
¼ cup pork/bacon fat
¼ cup Cotija cheese (American substitutes are feta
or parmesan)

½ lb. roast beef, pulled
2 cups sour cream
½ head of lettuce, chopped
2 avocados, sliced

Directions:

Knead the maseca and water in a bowl until it comes together, then let rest for 10 minutes. Form dough into small balls approximately 2 tablespoons each.

Flatten a little and then heat them in a pan without oil until golden. They should stay a little "gordita" (chubby) so you can pinch all around the edges to create a border.

After you pinch them, set them back in the heated pan, add the pork fat, beans, and beef and wait 1-2 minutes for the fat to melt.

Top with lettuce, cheese, sour cream, and avocado slices.

Martina

I am originally from Oaxaca. I am 35 years old, have four children, and am legally married. As a child, I went to school with my siblings and finished elementary school, which is not common for all girls my age. We were very poor. I dreamed of having toys like a doll or a tea party set growing up, but life was much different for me.

When I was seventeen, I met a man, and he became my boyfriend. Together we have a son who is now 14 years old. After eight years, I separated from him because he drank a lot of alcohol, and it was not a good situation for me and my son.

I met another man. He became my boyfriend and he wanted to get married. I was excited because we had only been together for a short time, yet he desired to pursue marriage with me. I felt desired and adored.

Soon after we were married, his character started to change, and we began having problems. He started to drink heavily and use drugs. He would get aggressive and violent to the point where I had to call the police. He had other problems with the authorities, and he was sent to jail for eight months. I wanted my children (we had three together and my older son) to be safe and not have anything to do with him. I didn't want his influence in their lives.

This was a very difficult time for me because I became a single mom. I worked from 6:00 AM to 5:00 PM to bring money into our home for survival. Though it was very difficult, I pressed on for my four children.

I came to Mujeres Nuevo Comienzo to ask Abuela Dorothy for food. I told her all my problems and because she has such a beautiful heart, she gave me some food and money. At the time, I didn't have a job, but she offered me one cleaning. I have been at MNC for eight months now. For me, it is a dream and a privilege for my kids to be here in daycare while I work.

Thank God for this job from Abuela. I am going to church with my children and teaching them His ways. I am happy my kids get to see the Love of God every day.

Author's Note:

Martina was not able to stay at MNC because she had a teenage boy. Teenage boys are considered young men, and they are not able to stay at the mission for safety reasons. They found her housing with a local missionary until she was able to get a house build. The mission provided financial support, childcare, work, dispenses (food allotments), transportation, and counseling. She is doing well and now works at another local mission in the area.

Ensalada Frio

Ingredients:

1 head of lettuce
½ cup carrot
1 can whole kernel corn
2 stalks celery
½ tomato
1 can tuna
1 chicken breast
½ cup mayo

¼ cup red onion
½ tsp chicken bouillon
Garlic salt to taste
Macaroni
Salt and pepper
Avocado
Oil of choice

Directions:

Dissolve the chicken bouillon in a pot of boiling water. Add the macaroni and allow it to cook for 8-10 minutes. Dice the lettuce, carrot, celery, and tomatoes and set aside.

In a small frying pan, add 1 tablespoon oil, onion, and garlic salt and cook until fragrant, add chicken and cook for 10 mins on each side. Shred chicken once cooked.

Combine the diced veggies, shredded chicken, corn, and tuna. Mix all ingredients together. Season with salt and pepper to taste. Top with avocado and enjoy.

Serve with tortilla chips or Ritz crackers.

Luciana

My name is Luciana. I am 26 years old, and I have two children. When I was seven years old my parents separated because my dad used a lot of drugs and alcohol. After they separated, my mother had three other boyfriends. I lived back and forth between my mom and dad; it was very unstable and frustrating.

I met a guy when I was 16 and we lived together for one year. I became pregnant with my beautiful daughter Maria, and it was such a gift when she was born. Soon after, I became pregnant with my son Matteo. When he was born, my boyfriend left me for another woman. He wanted nothing to do with me or our children. For a short time though, he was paying our rent so I could live and take care of our children. Eventually, the other woman insisted he should not pay rent any longer. I left without telling him and he arranged an Amber Alert in an attempt to find me.

I came to MNC because I had nowhere to go. My dad was in rehab and my mom was unable to help me because she had started using drugs and was very unstable as well. I stayed at the ministry for seven months and then left to try and live on my own but was unsuccessful. There are many expenses for a single mom. I went to live in my father's vacant house in Ensenada. Shortly after I arrived, he left rehab and came back with a partner. She did not want my children and me to live there. To help me, my dad rented me a house in Colonnette.

I was away from MNC for five years. I met a man, and we were together for a short time, maybe one month. He was threatening to kill me and wouldn't let me leave the house. He was using drugs non-stop. I was very depressed and wouldn't eat for days and weeks. My daughter was living with my mother, who was still using drugs. I couldn't get out of bed, so I called a psychologist. The doctor prescribed me pills for depression.

I felt at my lowest because I was in a bad situation once again and now needed medication just to function. I came back to MNC because I had no other place to go. I knew Abuela would accept me and love me.

Now I have realized God is always with me and He always provides for me. I can see in myself where I have matured. When I was here the first time, I had many problems with the women who lived here too, but I am changing and growing. I am working here at the restaurant training center.
A dream I have is to have my own house. I know God has not given it to me yet because I am not ready. This is helping me practice having patience and trusting God. I would like to help other women come out of hard, dark, and hopeless circumstances.

Author's Note:

Volunteers at the mission noted Luciana was at the mission for nine months during her last stay but she was desperate for companionship. She was doing well and then lost her focus. Unfortunately, not all women live in immediate victory when they leave MNC. Luciana chose to go back to prostitution and this summer narrowly escaped death from medical issues after an abortion. We have faith in God knowing the skills and love she received at the mission will help her in making the decision to continue fighting for peace and joy in her life.

> *"Have not I commanded you? Be strong and courageous; be not afraid, neither be thou dismayed:*
> *for the Lord thy God is with thee whithersoever thou goest."*

Joshua 1:9 (KJV)

Pozole Rojo

Ingredients:

12- 24 tostada shells
½ lb. precooked corn
1½ lb. chicken breast
⅔ cup of guajillo or ancho chile
½ onion
2 tomatoes

7 cloves of garlic
2 tbsp Knorr Suiza (chicken bouillon)
½ tbsp oregano
Salt to taste
Oil of choice

Suggested garnishes:

Chopped cilantro
White onion
Avocados

Limes
Sliced radish
Chopped cabbage

Directions:

Bring 5 qts of water to a boil and in a separate stockpot, put 3 cups of water to a boil. Heat chiles in the 3 cups of boiling water, covered for 10 minutes or until softened. Take out the chiles, remove stem and seeds. Soften the outside of the chile pods in a pan, careful not to burn. Place back into the 3 cups of hot water, cover, and let soak for 15 minutes.

Rinse the chicken and corn. Place them in a pot and cook for 30 mins. Once the chicken is cooked, remove the corn.

Put the chiles without water in a blender. Add tomato, garlic, onion, and cloves, then blend all the ingredients.

In a pan, put a tablespoon of oil; add the mixture and heat. Add bouillon with salt to taste. Finally, add the heated sauce to the chicken and water, add seasonings, add the corn back in and let simmer for an hour or until chicken is coming apart.

Serve soup with garnishes and tostada shells.

Renata

Hello, my name is Renata. My life has been a wild ride, but God is incredibly gracious and has saved me from a lot. In my 37 years on earth, I have survived many drug overdoses, gang-involved drive-by shootings, and a few suicide attempts. My parents cooked meth while I was growing up. My siblings and I helped with the business too.

I remember being raped by a man who came into our home to buy drugs from my parents when I was 12. I went to my mother for help, but instead she harshly responded with the cold words, "If this really happened, you asked for it, or you wanted it." I ran away and I promised never to see her again. Soon after, I started using drugs. Maybe I started using meth to hide the pain, or I may have decided to officially become part of the culture I was living in. Either way, it solidified my next 18 years of chaos.

Within the next year, I joined a southern California gang. When they needed parts for a car, I went to steal them. When drugs needed to be delivered, I delivered them. Many times, I had to run and hide from the police while I was working to avoid getting caught. Sometimes these would turn into high-speed car chases. I was arrested in 2004, at the age of 18, and served my first prison sentence because I was not able to flee from the police or convince them to let me go. A few years later, I met a man and fell in love. He was several years older and had just left prison, but I thought he was great. Our relationship started well but then he began to beat me. He was using drugs, and he was very controlling. He would not let me leave the house and would nail all the windows shut and put big locks on all the doors. He would lock me up, take all my clothes, and make me stay naked. When he came home, he would be high and sexually assault me, then burn me with his cigarette from the bottom of my feet to the top of my head.

One day, he came home and told me his plan was to bury me in the hole he was digging in the backyard. He said he would chop me up and then burn me. When he left the house for a walk, he did not realize he left the door open. I saw his father and begged him to help me, saying his son was going to kill me. He drove me to a friend's home, and she took me to the hospital.

I met another man with whom I lived for many years. He too became abusive, and at one point CPS got involved. I wasn't allowed to see my children for a time. I had four children with him and two older sons with another man. During my last pregnancy, my boyfriend wanted me to abort the baby. I was in the last trimester when we went to the abortion clinic. I'm not sure how, but the test said I wasn't pregnant and I'm glad my son was protected from death.

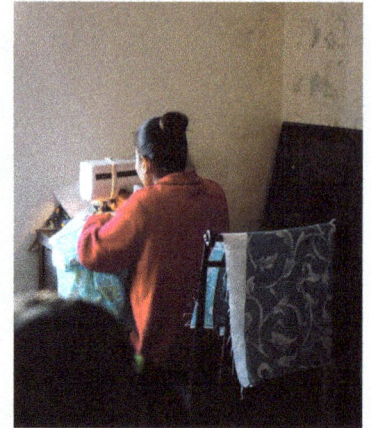

When I left that man in 2013, I went to get high to cope with the anger and hurt. I relapsed again and lost my children again. Others jeered, saying, "The kids are better off without you. You are nothing. You've tried to get clean many times, but you always give up and give in."

In June of 2014, I fell into a deep depression. I would sleep all day long, feeling worthless. I decided I needed to end my life. I had a handgun and a plan. Before I could pull the trigger, my brother texted me to see how I was doing. I told him I could not take it any longer. I had lost my children, I was a drug addict, and I did not want to live to see another day of the painful life I had created. He begged me to give life one more chance, and to come to Mexico and visit him.

> For though we live in the world, we do not wage war as the world does. The weapons we fight with are not the weapons of the world. On the contrary, they have divine power to demolish strongholds. We demolish arguments and every pretension that sets itself up against the knowledge of God, and we take captive every thought to make it obedient to Christ.
>
> 2 Corinthians 10:3-5 (NIV)

I decided to go visit him and then went to a mission he wanted me to go to. When I arrived, this lady named Dorothy hugged me and told me she had been praying for me for years. At first, I thought she was crazy. But I quickly became accustomed to her encouragement. She would say things like "You are amazing! God has great plans for you! You have wonderful gifts! Look how well you did!" The only words I remembered hearing previously were that I was worthless, I deserved being raped, I was never going to become anything. Dorothy's consistent encouragement, my new friend Maria's wisdom, and God's love helped me change my thinking.

After a year of being clean, I decided to visit my children in California. I thought I was strong enough to be around previous friends. But I wasn't. In less than a week, I started using again. My friends and my brother back in Mexico helped me but I was worried Dorothy would not let me return. Surprisingly, she did it with open arms and no lectures. I had never felt this manner of forgiveness before.

Here I have learned to have compassion for others, to tame my anger, and most importantly, that I am capable of having friends. In the past, somebody always wanted something from me, and I wanted something from them. We used each other. Now, I know I can be a good friend and genuinely love people. At the end of the day, I thank God for this place.

Author's Note:

Renata lived in Vicente Guerrero for a few years before returning to the U.S. She still has struggles with her former life but has found victory in many areas. She is now living in the States, where she is able to be part of her children's lives.

Red Enchiladas

Ingredients:

4 cups shredded cooked chicken
20 corn tortillas (see recipe)
1 cup of tomato sauce
½ cup california dry chiles
½ cup of cheese
2 garlic cloves
2 cups of oil

½ tsp paprika
¼ onion
2 cups of water
Salt to taste
Sour cream to taste
½ head chopped iceberg lettuce

Directions:

Preheat the oven to 350°F.

Fry the chiles in a saucepan with 1 tsp oil of choice. Once the chile is darkened in color, place in a blender with onion, garlic, paprika, and salt. Blend until smooth. Set aside.

Heat two cups of oil in a small pot until the oil is warm. Submerge the tortilla fully into oil for 15 seconds. Remove and submerge the same tortilla into the tomato sauce and lay onto a baking sheet. Place two tbsp shredded chicken into the tortilla and roll the tortilla. Place in a baking pan. Continue until all tortillas have been used. Pour remaining tomato sauce over the enchiladas and sprinkle with shredded cheese. Bake for 15 minutes or until bubbly and golden. Serve with sour cream and shredded lettuce on top.

Corn Tortillas

Ingredients:

2 cups (240 grams) corn flour
1½ to 2 cups hot water

1 teaspoon sea salt

Directions:

Place corn flour and salt into a mixing bowl. Slowly add hot water ½ cup at a time. Knead for 10 minutes or until the texture is similar to playdough. Cover the dough and allow it to rest for five minutes. Divide dough into 2-tbsp balls. Press using a tortilla press, pie plate, or rolling pin. Heat griddle or frying pan to medium/high heat. Cook the tortilla for about 40-60 seconds per side, flipping it once speckled brown spots begin to appear on the bottom of the tortilla. The tortillas will likely bubble up while cooking, especially on the second side, which is a good sign! Once it is cooked, transfer the tortilla to a tortilla warmer or a bowl with a clean kitchen towel inside to wrap the tortillas, so they do not dry out.

When I came to Baja California at 19, I met the father of my first daughter. I found myself pregnant during our relationship. One time, I had talked to another man while I was with the father of my baby. He accused me of

cheating on him and left me alone, pregnant. I was on my own, working to try and provide for me and my baby. When my employers found out I was six months pregnant, they told me I could not work anymore. With nowhere to go, I reluctantly moved in with my brother and sister-in-law again. It was fine until she didn't want me living with them and eating their food. I went to the hospital for a checkup and met a nurse who asked me to take care of her children. I decided to take her offer. She let me move in with her. She became like a mom to me, caring about me and giving me hugs and loving me. She helped me be a mom to my daughter. I was excited but also so emotional, since I was about to start parenting all by myself.

Later that year, while I was working for the nurse, I met a man and became pregnant again. He promised me the world but then he didn't stay. Once again, I found myself alone and feeling heartbroken, knowing I was about to bring another child into my broken life. The feelings of failure were intense. I was considering an abortion, but people walked beside me and encouraged me to keep my baby. Praise God. I am so grateful I made the decision to keep my baby.

The nurse I worked for left for the United States and she brought me here to Mujeres Nuevo Comienzo so I would have a place to stay. The nurse eventually came back to Vicente Guerrero, but I decided to stay at Mujeres Nuevo Comienzo because I grew up so inexperienced not knowing much language, cooking, or God.

Although it is difficult to live with many women, I am learning the language and life skills. We are not held against our will here and many times I left because I thought I could find a better life for my family.

While I was searching, I would try to go back to my brother but again, I was not welcomed by my sister-in-law. I would return to Mujeres Nuevo Comienzo, and every time, I was received with loving arms and I felt wanted.

It took me many times of leaving and searching to see this mission was an open door for me. It was difficult for me to understand what they were sharing at church or read the Word of God because I didn't speak much Spanish, just my dialect from Oaxaca. I could feel the overwhelming love and presence of God even without knowing the language. I have been abundantly blessed to have work and be supported by MNC. I now have a house for myself and my daughters. I am very grateful for the mission that builds homes for us. When I first walked into my house, I was so overwhelmed by peace. Life is better, I am blessed.

Author's Note:

Lia lived at MNC for three years and now has a house build. She mentioned she lived in an orphanage for a few years. In Mexico, families are legally allowed to surrender their children to orphanages if they cannot afford to feed and care for them. The goal is that those children will one day be reunited with their family when they are able to resume the ability to meet basic needs.

Flautas

Ingredients:

For the flautas:
20 corn tortillas (see recipe)
2 potatoes
3-4 chicken breasts
Salt and pepper
2 cups oil of choice

1 tbsp butter
½ onion, chopped
¼ tsp paprika
Toothpicks
2 cloves of garlic
2 tomatoes

Topping:

1 head lettuce, shredded
1 cup sour cream

Queso fresco or grated Monterey jack cheese
Optional: salsa (see page 49)

Directions:

Heat a pot full of water on high. Cut potatoes into cubes and put them into boiling water. Allow to cook until soft. Once soft, strain the potatoes, add butter, paprika, and salt to taste, and set aside.

Fill another pot with water and let it boil. Cut chicken breasts in half and boil until fully cooked. Strain water and shred chicken. Add 1 tsp oil to a saucepan and heat on medium heat.

Chop onion and tomatoes and press garlic. Sauté until brown. Add shredded chicken breasts and brown. Remove from heat and add potatoes. In a large saucepan, heat two cups of oil of choice on medium heat. In one tortilla, place 2 tbsp of mixture.

Roll the tortilla up and place a toothpick to hold the roll in place. Add to the oil and allow it to cook until brown for approximately 1 minute. Flip to allow the other side to brown. Remove from the heat and remove the toothpick. Repeat. Top with cheese, sour cream, and shredded lettuce.

Ximena

Hello. My name is Ximena. I am 40 years old, and I have five children. Sixteen years ago, I married my children's father. He was addicted to drugs. There were many times he acted out in violence towards me. The last day we spent in the home, he became very angry. I do not remember a lot about the event, but he tried to strangle me. One of my daughters ran to the neighbor's house to get help. They called the police, who came and took my children and me to the mission. I knew it was impossible to continue living a life in which my children and I were exposed to physical and emotional abuse. I am happy we found a place of refuge where we could all be safe.

I accepted the help. The truth is, I do not regret coming to this place. It is a Christian place, and it has helped me and my children to stay healthy. The living environment is very favorable. After seven months, they gave me the joyous news that I was going to receive a house. Firstly, I thank God and Abuela. To date, I am very happy and grateful for everything and to see my children are also happy in their new home. Praise God.

Author's Note:

Ximena came to MNC in 2021. When she arrived, her older daughters were 15 and 14 years old. One of the volunteers said they kept to themselves and barely spoke. In the summer of 2021, a volunteer team with several teenagers who spoke Spanish came, and they became friends with the girls. They helped them come out of their protective shell simply by being friends. They are still doing well and volunteer at MNC and another local ministry.

When they received a home, Ximena found employment at a local berry field and would get up at 2:00 am to make tamales to sell before working in the fields. Late in 2022, she was diagnosed with tuberculosis and has been unable to work. She dreams of having her own kitchen one day, where she can sell her tamales. For now, the ministry is helping with bills as needed, sending food home with the older daughters, and supporting care for the younger brothers. Overall, the family is doing well. They still attend church and are continuing to grow and heal.

Mexican Pizza

The Dough:

1 cup warm water (110°F/45°C)
1 (0.25 ounce) package active dry yeast
1 tsp white sugar

2½ cups bread flour
2 tbsp olive oil
1 tsp salt

Toppings:

1 can pizza sauce
2 cups grated cheese
2 jalapeños
½ cup chopped bacon

½ cup chopped ham
½ cup ground chorizo sausage
½ cup prepared beans *(see page 49 for recipe)*
or canned beans

Directions:

Preheat the oven to 450°F. Pour one cup of warm water into a bowl. Add yeast and sugar and allow to rise for 10 minutes. Add flour, oil, and salt to the yeast mixture; beat until smooth. Pour onto a floured surface and roll into desired shape.

Heat a frying pan and cook ground chorizo until browned. Repeat for the bacon. Spread the tomato sauce all over the surface of the pizza crust. Cube the ham and bacon and place over the tomato sauce. Add beans and chop jalapeños into pieces if desired to remove seeds for a less spicy pizza. Top with cheese and cook on 450°F until the cheese is bubbly and the bottom of the pizza crust is golden brown. Cool and slice into pieces to share!

Amelia

I am the mother of two children. I believe sharing testimonies and life experiences is important for growth in myself and others. In my life, I have been through many struggles and battles. Right now, they feel easier to share but once it was very difficult to live through. I had a beautiful family, and everything was destroyed when my husband got sick; all I could see was torn pieces. I didn't know how to put my family back together. When I tried to do everything in my own strength, I felt hopeless. I didn't have truth and hope: Jesus Christ.

He that dwelleth in the secret place of the Most High shall abide under the shadow of the Almighty. I will say of the Lord, He is my refuge and my fortress; my God; in him I will trust.

Psalm 91:1-2 (KJV)

My husband was very sick and we searched for ways to heal from his disease. He had five operations, chemotherapy, and the amputation of his leg at the knee, among many other things. Even through the sickness we fiercely fought day and night. In one of our fights, we decided to look to God to help us. We went to a church but didn't continue going after a few visits. We always went back home and started to argue or fight again. We continued the same fighting and eventually he lost the battle to cancer and passed away.

Our lives were so broken. My son asked me when his daddy would return to us. It destroyed my soul, not being able to calm the suffering. What I experienced led me to make a decision to travel to Baja California, Mexico. I came to live and work there.

The years passed and I met the father of my daughter. He wanted to play games with my feelings. I met Abuela and she invited us to church, but I refused to accept. She extended the invitation many times and many times I said no.

When my daughter was born, I made the hard decision to go live at MNC. Thank God and our Lord Jesus Christ, I accepted Him as my savior. I was baptized and I have God in my heart. Maybe if I had met God sooner my life would have been different. It is not in my time but in His.

> "So do not fear, for I am with you; do not be dismayed, for I am your God. I will strengthen you and help you; I will uphold you with my righteous right hand. All who rage against you will surely be ashamed and disgraced; those who oppose you will be as nothing and perish. Though you search for your enemies, you will not find them. Those who wage war against you will be as nothing at all. For I am the Lord your God who takes hold of your right hand and says to you, Do not fear; I will help you." Isaiah 41:10-13 (NIV)

Author's Note:

Amelia lived at the mission for 11 months and received the blessing of a house build. She currently works as a chef at MNC and is doing well.

Dark Mole

Ingredients:

4 guajillo chiles
1 pasilla chiles
2 ancho chiles
2 cloves of garlic
1 banana
1 clove garlic
1 cinnamon stick
50 g (2 oz.) toasted sesame seeds
50 g (2 oz.) raisin
50 g (2 oz.) dried pumpkin seeds

2 ground Ritz crackers
¼ dark chocolate bar
¼ liter oil of choice
2 roasted red tomatoes
½ onion
¼ tsp cumin
½ tsp pepper
1 tsp salt
1 pound chicken of choice (breasts, thighs, legs)

Directions:

Heat a frying pan with 1 tsp oil. Sprinkle chicken with salt and pepper and cook in the oil until fully cooked.

Heat a medium size frying pan on medium heat. Place all the chiles in the pan and fry until they are browned. Add pressed garlic, chopped onion, and remaining ingredients and cook until they are fried well.

Add the ingredients from the frying pan into the blender.

Blend until you have a smooth sauce, approximately 1.5 minutes. Pour the sauce back into the pan and add the chicken to boil before serving.

Top with sesame seeds and serve with rice.

Fernanda

I was born in Baja California. I was an unplanned baby and from a young age I was labeled as unwanted. I was neglected and abandoned. I struggled in school and struggled to understand things. I never had a relationship with my dad and was solely raised by my mother. When I was six years old, I remember being touched inappropriately. When my mom would work in the fields, she would leave me home with my sister and her boyfriend. I was constantly molested from the ages of six to 11.

When I was 11, we moved to Oaxaca. I was struggling; I was tired and weak. My mom asked me why I was always sleeping. She thought I was pregnant, but I finally shared with her the years of darkness I had endured. I had never told my mom because my abuser threatened constantly that if I did tell there would be consequences for me and my family. It felt freeing to finally talk about the abuse. (Fernanda did not share how her mother responded to the news.)

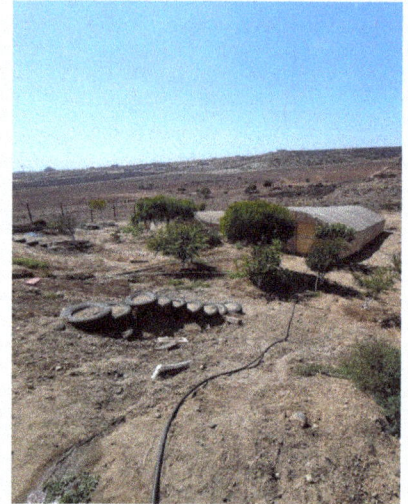

Years later, when I was 21, I returned to Baja California and started working in the camps (fields). I met a man who often shared his lunch with me. I had always wanted a man in my life because I didn't have a father. We moved in after only a few weeks of being together. A year later, I got pregnant. My first year with my boyfriend was good. He was a hard worker and kind to me. He would drink just for fun during parties. He started drinking more and more and left me very often but came back. He stopped working and started using drugs, and I had to financially support us.

When our first baby was 18 months old, I got pregnant again. My boyfriend was getting worse and worse. My mother-in-law lived next door and she watched me all day. He would come home drugged up, searching for clues to accuse me of sleeping with someone else. He would strip my clothing off and search for evidence I hadn't slept with anyone. I was treated like garbage for five years. I vividly remember going to the streets asking for food because we had nothing. Since he was consumed by drugs, I could not bear the thought of him watching the two babies while I left for work, so I stayed home and found ways to survive.

Years went by and the abuse continued. I remember one evening vividly. He was so mad at me he grabbed my hair and twisted it with such force it took me violently to the floor. He proceeded to kick me hard in the stomach until I peed. He then humiliated me more by telling my kids to look at me and see how disgusting I was.

One day, I decided to stand up to him. I was so exhausted from the abuse and lack of love. There was no food in my house, no water (in order to have water, it must be purchased from a delivery company), no coffee… nothing. When I expressed my frustration, he picked up a stick and beat my head and neck and continued on to my whole body. When he stopped, I fled, and a stranger took me to MNC. When I arrived, we went and filed a police report, but my boyfriend had already been there and filed his own report stating I had abandoned my children. He received custody of both of our boys.

When I would attempt to go visit my children, my mother-in-law would demand payment before I could see my babies. I brought them a birthday cake and she threw it onto the floor. She would hide the children behind her and threaten me with a broom. I was called many ugly things like a dog, and I believed it for many years.

I almost returned to my husband, believing if I did, I could be a mother to my children. My husband threatened that if I ever returned, he would kill me and bury me. I lived at Mujeres Nuevo Comienzo for three years and in transition for one year. I had a job in Vicente Guerrerro at a material shop. I loved my job and the people there loved me. When I was at MNC, I started to see myself as valuable. I was always told I had no worth and no value from childhood through my marriage.

As I studied the Bible and learned different skills, I started to see that I can learn things, I am not a piece of trash, and I am not a mistake.

Author's Note:

Fernanda was not able to bridge the lies with her children. They still believe she is a person they do not want in their lives. Recently, though, she received another chance of motherhood with her new baby girl born in May 2023. She received a home build and her, her baby, and her new partner are living there near the ministry. She is doing well.

Molito

Ingredients:

3 guajillo chiles
2 cloves of garlic
¼ tsp cumin
½ tsp oregano
3 red tomatoes
Salt

½ onion, chopped
½ lb. chicken thighs
or legs
5 cups water
1½ cups maseca or
corn flour

Directions:

Bring 4 cups water to a boil. Add the chicken and boil until thoroughly cooked, about 20 minutes. Take the meat out of water and set aside the water from the boiled chicken; this becomes the chicken water.

In another pot, to create a salsa mixture, boil the tomatoes, chiles, onion, and garlic in 1 cup water until cooked. Place mixture in blender and blend until smooth. Set aside.

Add the corn flour into a hot pot over medium heat. Add the chicken water slowly while whisking very quickly to prevent it from sticking. You want the texture to be quite liquid. Allow to simmer as you whisk. Add the salsa mixture into the corn flour mixture. Mix in the cumin and oregano. Add salt to taste. Pour mix over the chicken. Eat with rice.

Natalia

Hello. My name is Natalia. I have three children and I am 36 years old. I was born in Ensenada, but my family returned to Guadalajara shortly after I was born. I have 13 siblings. My mom was very loving and was an amazing mother. My father was cold, was not very sensitive, and didn't embrace or show affection to us as his children.

My father was always in our house, but he was distant from my family and stayed because of his marital obligation to my mother. When I was 12, my older sister got cancer and my mother had to go be with her in the hospital. This change left me in charge of all the other children. While my mom was gone, my dad started doing very bad things like drinking a lot and having relationships with other women. My parents never separated but I saw my father become more aggressive and stop providing for my family.

I didn't know what it was to be loved by my father. As each of us turned 18, we would leave with the first boyfriend we got because my father forbade us to have boyfriends. It was our way to escape.

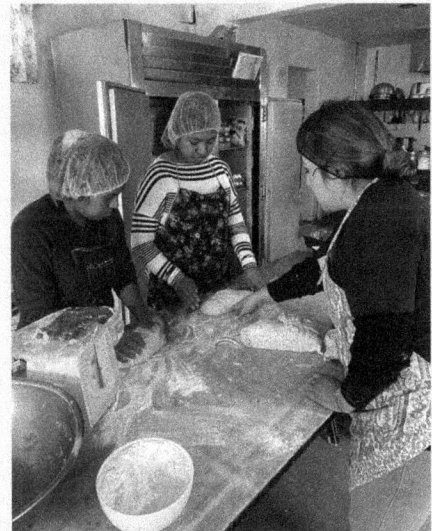

After eight days of living with my boyfriend, I discovered he was living and sleeping with someone else. I was only 18 and he was 30 years old. I called my mom, and she told me to come home but I assumed what my dad would think and say. I was planning on leaving but then I found out I was pregnant with his baby.

It was a very difficult and emotional pregnancy for me. I was struggling deeply because I was dealing with feelings of hurt and I didn't want the baby. My boyfriend kept promising to stop being with other women and I believed him. I stayed because of the baby but it was not a happy or loving relationship. Although I didn't want the baby the whole pregnancy, as soon as I saw my son, I fell in love with him.

Eventually, I left with my son to go live with my parents, but I had no future living there. I conceded and returned to my boyfriend because I had been brainwashed to believe I needed him and could be nothing without him. He continued to make empty promises, swearing he would quit his addictions and his rendezvous with other women. Every time, these tugged at my heart because I desperately wanted to believe him. I bought his lies, choosing to stay, and soon I became pregnant again. I left when the baby was born but he found me and threatened me with lawyers and court hearings.

I gave him what he wanted, and he told me he wanted to be a father to our little boys. My second son became very sick and needed blood transfusions. We were in the hospital for three months during the treatments. I held my son in my arms as the doctor told me he might not live. I cried because so many times when I was pregnant and depressed, I didn't want him but, in that moment, I hurt in a way I had never felt before. I realized I wanted him so badly.

This was a time where God brought me to my lowest – a place of desperation. Through this time, the father of my babies was present and helped me get through all the difficulty. The support he showed gave me hope that our future could be better. I returned to him once my son was well, believing yet again we could be a family.

Nothing changed. My children and I were living an ugly life of no peace. I was bitter from feeling rejected, my kids saw and lived it as well. The father continued to spiral down a deep dark path of drugs and women. One time when I was cleaning a family farm to make money, I found the drugs and told him I was going to call the cops. I do not know if he was dealing or just consuming. He locked me and my children in the house and took my phone for one week because he was afraid I would turn him in to the police.

When the neighbor was out planting his garden, I screamed through the bathroom window for help, and he came and unlocked the door. I went to go live with my sister and found out I was pregnant yet again. I was hiding from him but one day when I was at a doctor's appointment, he found me. He threatened my brother-in-law and my sister, saying he would kill them if I didn't go back to live with him.

I decided not to go back with him, but once I had the baby, he tracked me down in the hospital. He found me every time. I discovered he had tabs on me everywhere I went. I didn't want to live anymore. I lived in desperation, darkness, and fear. I had no hope or life. He tormented me by calling me on different phone numbers all day, all night, and stalking me.

My cousin tried to help by buying me tickets to fly from Guadalajara to Baja California. As we were headed to the airport, he found out and caused us to be unable to get on our flights. We got on a bus and traveled three days and nights with my three little children. When I arrived at Mujeres Nuevo Comienzo, they told me it was confidential and I was safe, but I trusted nobody.

When I arrived, the road was muddy, and the town was ugly. Abuela told me I was not allowed a phone and I said, "Thank you for your help but I'm going to go." She asked me to consider it a little longer. I decided I'd sleep there for the night and leave the next day because I trusted nobody. I called my cousin the next day to come and pick me up because I was ready to leave. Dorothy had a loving talk with me and shared the ways I was safe there and having no communication with the outside world for a little was part of creating safety for me. I changed my mind and decided to stay.

I started working after three months and it built my confidence. I had lived many years with the inability to believe more than what my children's father repeatedly told me – that I was good for nothing. I saved up and bought my land and a beautiful gift of a house was given to me. I get to work at the restaurant training center and provide for my family. I have watched Abuela love other women and guide them through their pain. God is teaching me how to love and help other women who have also been through difficult situations because I can relate. God is my hope.

Author's Note:

Natalia was a waitress for MNC and now works in the valley.

Mexican Frijoles

Ingredients:

2 quarts of water
2 tsp oil (bacon fat is best for flavor)
¼ chopped onion
2 cloves of garlic
Salt to taste

3 cups beans of choice (dry, not canned)
Optional: Use ¼ cup bacon fat for frying and mashing the beans to add flavor.

Directions:

Thoroughly wash 3 cups of beans in water. Once cleaned, add beans and salt to a large soup pot and add 2 quarts of water. Allow to boil and then turn down heat to allow a slow simmer for 1.5-2 hours. After 2 hours, the beans should be soft. Strain them and set aside.

In a frying pan, add oil, chopped onion, and pressed garlic, and brown. Once the onion is browned, add beans and mash until smooth. Serve warm with rice, tortillas, and meat of choice!

Elena

My childhood was sad but at the same time good. It was good when my sisters and I lived with my grandmother. We lived there for six years without my parents. I was seven when they came for us. My grandmother was sick and could no longer care for us. The saddest and most difficult thing in my life was losing my grandmother. It was so hard watching her slowly die. It was a very sad day for me to lose someone I loved so dearly and who I knew loved me.

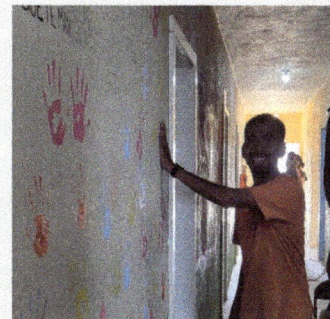

Life was different living with my parents. My father and I got along well, but the relationship with my mother was not very good. I don't know the reason she never treated me well. The only thing I know is I should not hold a grudge against her because she's my mother and I love her even though she has treated me with no love.

When I was older, I met a man whom I fell in love with. My first experience of love from a man was something so beautiful because we supported each other, we made decisions together. It was real love: we chose each other, we wanted to be together.

Eventually, the love turned to abuse. He no longer paid attention to me and our son. He spent a lot of his time with another woman, and he didn't come home or support us with money. In order for us to eat, my mother-in-law helped us with groceries. She didn't like the way he treated us. Thankfully, she did what she could to help and support us. She is the one who led me to the decision to come to MNC. I needed to be free from the constant physical pain and the lack of care from my husband. From the time I got here, I have been sustained by the Word of God – reading the Bible, praying, asking God to give me the strength I needed to leave. My goal – my dream – is to get ahead with my son to give him what he needs.

I thank all the people who have helped me and supported me. I thank Sister Susie, Abuela, Emily and her family, Brother Jorge, and all the women who have supported me in everything. Thank you and may God bless you at all times.

Author's Note:

Elena did not finish the program at MNC and left to live with her mother-in-law. We pray for the best for her.

Bistec Ranchero con Frijoles (Steak with Beans)

Ingredients:

2 lbs. steak	1 clove garlic
3 tomatoes	Salt
1 chile	Oil
½ yellow onion	1 can beans of choice

Directions:

Chop the meat and the vegetables.

In a pan, heat some oil, then sauté the meat in the pan until preferred temperature is reached.

In another pan, heat 1 tablespoon oil and add chopped garlic and diced onions. When onions are translucent, add tomatoes and chile, cooking until soft. Remove from heat. Combine with cooked meat.

Cook beans with desired method. Serve together.

Josefina

I grew up very poor with my five sisters and my mom and dad. Both of my parents worked in the vegetable fields. My father was an alcoholic and I often watched as he continuously beat my mom. I was very frightened of him. When he got drunk and began a rampage of beating my mom, my siblings and I would slip out through the window and flee. I was intentional about taking my little sister with me to protect her.

Sometimes, it was days until my mom came to find us to let us know it was safe to come home. Out of all her children, I always felt like my mom didn't really like me very much. I'm not sure why; we just never connected. She wasn't one to give affection, hugs, or affirmations. Nor were those things ever shown in our house.

When I was 13 years old, my older sister's boyfriend moved into our home. He wanted to be with me and would coerce and threaten me into being with him sexually. My sister would kick me out of the house when my mom would leave for four to five days at a time. I remember being so hungry and trying to find food. I would beg for food in the streets and look in the garbage to see if there was anything to fill my stomach. I was sick of being treated this way. My sister and I had one big giant fight because I decided to stand up for myself for the way she was treating me. When my mom found out about the fight, she got angry at me because my sister was pregnant, and she said I was out of line. I felt betrayed by my mom, as though my parents were always mad at me, and my sister could do no wrong. I felt like I couldn't live in that house anymore and it was time for me to leave, but I had nowhere to go.

I began working at a nearby store and one day, a 13-year-old boy came in to buy a soda. When he left, I realized he hadn't paid enough, so I ran after him to let him know he needed to pay more. I was 14 years old at the time. The conversation turned from what I thought it would be – he invited me into his house because his parents were not home. I knew it was a bad decision, but I went and I stayed with him. I didn't want to go home to my family.

When his parents came home days later, they found out who my parents were, and they discussed what would happen with us next. My parents negotiated with them and sold me to his parents. We got married. We had a party to "celebrate" but I was not excited; I had been given no option. I quickly became a slave to my mother-in-law. When they woke up, they wanted breakfast made. I had to wash the laundry and make sure the house was clean. I was the maid, cook, and sitter. I wanted to leave but my mom didn't want me in her house either. I did not believe I had any other options; they owned me.

Eventually, my husband started treating me like a slave as well. He would beat me, and his parents encouraged it. They told me I was useless and I deserved to be "put in my place". I didn't know how to clean or cook but I learned very quickly. The pressure and abuse were debilitating and terrifying. I couldn't decide what was worse: witnessing my parents' tumultuous relationship or being enslaved and abused. One day when my husband started beating me, I decided to flee. I went to my parents' home. My mom took me in for the moment but said I had to return because the family had paid for me.

I desperately searched for help but everywhere I turned I was rejected and unwanted.

Upon returning to my "owners," they made me work in the fields harvesting onions. They told me I had to pay off the money they had invested in me. I was 15 and pregnant. I was picking in the fields when two weeks before my due date, I started bleeding. I was rushed to the hospital and had an emergency C-section. The C-section cost 15,000 pesos. I was sent home with my baby and an incubator where he slept for 15 days. I found myself staring at him as he slept, mesmerized by his peace. My husband and his parents didn't want me or the baby. When the baby was one month old, I had no choice but to put him on my back and work in the fields again to pay off my debt.

One day, I was at home sitting on a chair with my son. My husband randomly started to beat me repeatedly on my head. The incident played out in slow motion in my mind. As I tried to protect my son from the beating, he slipped through my hands to the floor, hurting his neck during the fall. We had to spend time in the hospital as he recovered. The time in the hospital was mentally exhausting but provided a few moments of peace while my son healed. This added even more debt to the amount I now owed to the family.

Soon, I was pregnant again and my husband wanted to get rid of the baby. I struggled heavily because I didn't want any of this. He just continued to come home drunk and beat me. His mother told him she saw me with another man and made accusations of the baby not being her son's. One night, he came home more drunk than normal and tried to kill me with a machete because he was convinced I was being unfaithful.

I fled with my son to my husband's sister's house. He came looking for me and once we talked it out, I returned because I believed I had nowhere to go. He hated me and our second son. Honestly, I hated myself. My husband and I moved out and started renting a house even though we had no money. He didn't work; he just drank all day and started to have many relationships with other women. He would come home and beat me black and purple. Sometimes during the worst of the beatings, he would try to kill me with a knife or bite me.

I was the only one working, but after delivering our third child (a daughter) by C-section, I could not work for a bit. My boys were on the streets begging for money or trying to clean cars. Sometimes, they would come back with enough to buy one bag of maseca with which to make tortillas. When they came back empty handed, we had no food or water. The lady we rented from saw me one day and gave me some tortillas, instructing me not to give them to my husband. I was terrified of him; he would eat any food we did happen to have. I fell into suicidal thoughts and many times considered walking out into traffic. Sometimes, I wished my husband would just kill me during one of his rages. I had no hope and no future. I held on because I had children who needed a mother.

The landlord went to a nearby church and when my daughter got very sick, she invited me to come with her to get prayer for my daughter. I accepted the invitation because I heard they handed out clothing and I had nothing but a great need. We each had one outfit. I didn't know God at all, but my heart was touched there, and I prayed, "If there is actually a God, would You save me from this?" I began to go regularly with her. He would accuse me of only going to have sex with men behind the church. When he came home drunk, I hid all the knives. The landlord told me about Mujeres Nuevo Comienzo and said she was going to report my husband and the social services would take my children because they were in danger too. She told me about this place and how they help shelter women, help them heal, help them find jobs, and help them buy land to have their own house one day.

When I arrived at MNC, I was angry. I had nightmares and would wake up screaming, believing my abuser was coming into the gates to get me. I didn't understand Spanish because I grew up only knowing my dialect. I hid in my shell. Slowly over time, as Abuela prayed for me, my walls started to come down. Little by little, God began to transform my life. For the next two to three years, as I had time away from a life of torture, I was able to change. I had been in a prison of abuse for so long it took me a while to learn to allow God in.

Here, I learned how to love my children. I never grew up being hugged or loved. All the years with my husband, I was used, abused, and tortured, I had no idea how to love or what real love was. I was told I was worth less than a dirty rag, but here, I have learned in the eyes of God, I am precious. I no longer live in fear of being beat up. I have a Father who hears me and gives me peace when my fear creeps in.

God radically changed my life and I thank Him with all my heart. I want to tell all the women who are here: do not get discouraged because in this place there is blessing and prosperity. I also want to thank Abuela and the Americans for helping me build my beautiful house. For me, it was a great blessing God has given me, and He also guided me to the right path. Finally, I want to thank all the people who have supported me. This is my testimony. Thanks for everything. Blessings to all.

Author's Note:

Her older boys were able to go work in the U.S. and she and her younger children live in Vicente Guerrero in a house build she was blessed with. She is doing well and is a good mother.

Spanish Eggs

Ingredients:

¼ onion
6 eggs
4 dried California peppers
1 clove of garlic

3 red tomatoes
½ tsp oil
Salt and pepper to taste

Directions:

Heat a frying pan and oil lightly. Crack all eggs into a bowl, add salt and pepper and whisk thoroughly. In a small pot, place your chile and tomatoes and add enough water so the tomatoes don't touch the bottom of the pan. Boil the water for 2 minutes. Transfer the tomatoes and chiles into a blender and blend until smooth. Add the mixture back into the frying pan with eggs and let simmer altogether for 4 minutes. Enjoy.

Roma

While growing up, I never lacked anything of the physical kind. We weren't poor; my parents did well. My dad was a king to me — my best friend — and I could talk to him about anything. My mom, on the other hand, treated me harshly. For some reason, I wasn't the daughter she wanted; she seemed to detest me. She was a homemaker and a perfectionist, and I was anything but perfect in her eyes and she treated me as such.

My parents fought around the clock (and still do). As I grew, I did not want to live in constant hostility any longer. As much as I loved my father, I could not live in such turmoil. When I was 17, I met a 27-year-old man and started seeing him just to get out of my parents' house. It wasn't for love, just for an escape. Living with him was not good, but I became accustomed to it. He beat me and treated me like a dog — unwanted rubbish in the street — but if I had gone home to my mother, it would have been just as bad. There was no good reason in my mind to leave.

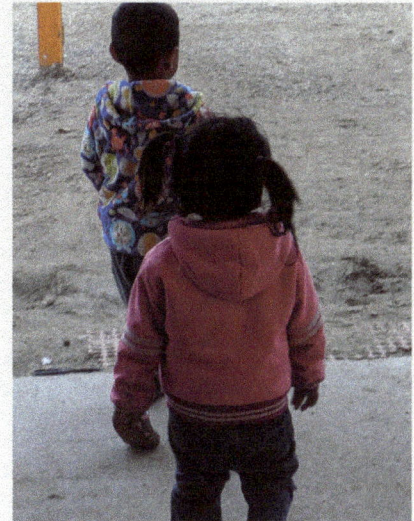

After a year with him, I became pregnant with my son, the love of my life. We were two adults raising a child, but we didn't really have a relationship with each other; we were more like bad roommates. I was so young and innocent, I didn't know he was using drugs until we had been together for a while. When I turned 19, I started using the drugs along with him. Unfortunately, it became an all-consuming addiction, and I flushed 12 years of my life down the drain. Eventually, we moved to Tecate looking for a better life, but soon after, my husband went missing.

For 20 days, I walked the streets of Tijuana, where he was last seen, looking everywhere for him. Where I come from, it is common for drug dealers to go missing. You never know if someone will be found chopped to pieces in a bag or found alive but nearly dead. Although he was never found, the police declared him dead. Some still accuse me of participating in his disappearance, assuming I had something to do with it, even my son. We were both dealing drugs and it was not a good life.

After I lost my husband, I went to work at a Toyota dealership. I was clean and working hard to have a good life. The money was good, but I knew dealing was more profitable. The greed took hold, and I went back to dealing. My son wanted a better life. He was still grieving the loss of his father and frustrated with me for selling drugs. He continued to blame me for his dad being gone. He said if I didn't change, then he would go and live with my parents in Durango. I tried to change. I deeply wanted to be a good person; I knew that the life I was living wasn't what I should be doing.

I stopped using and dealing and we moved to Durango to make a change, but there was very little work there for me. My son and I moved in with my parents, my brother, his wife, and their children. They all lived in the same house and none of them worked. It was up to me to care for them, so I started working in the tomato fields. I had allergies to vegetables and was quite miserable. I made 700 pesos a week [depending on the exchange rate, 700 pesos roughly 43 U.S. dollars]. It was not enough to feed and take care of all of us.

I connected with a childhood friend in San Quintin, who told me there was a lot of work for me there. My friends gave me enough money to go, so I went to make another attempt at a better life. I hated it there; it was so ugly. The whole time I was in Durango with my family I didn't touch drugs. As soon as I got to San Quintin, I started using drugs again, maybe out of sheer sadness because the town seemed as miserable as I felt.

I was living with a friend while I tried to get established in the town, and when she found out I was using again she kicked me out. Thankfully, my friend's uncle allowed me to rent a house from him. It was a very lonely life for me. I desperately wanted to quit, but I couldn't; I kept using and worked very hard to keep it a secret. I had a dealer who befriended me and helped me cope with my loneliness. Soon, he became my boyfriend. He would give me drugs when I was sick from withdrawal because I didn't have any money for myself. I realized I had more than I needed, and I asked a friend if he knew anyone who needed drugs so I could get some money. He told me, "Everyone is using, and you could easily sell it anywhere."

Eventually, my boyfriend discovered what I was doing. He was very angry with me, and instead of me stopping I went even deeper into selling. I began making and selling my own drugs. I started managing many drug accounts and eventually had people selling for me. If caught, I wouldhave been in deep trouble. Commonly, if dealers cross into other people's drug dealing areas, very serious repercussions take place. I kept going, pushing harder to sell more and gain clientele. I earned official status selling crystal meth in this area. I was the one everyone came to. I went as far as selling in Ensenada. My boyfriend and I had joined together and had a hub and a main office where we both sold from. He sold from the storefront, and I delivered. This continued for 10 months.

I remember the day I lost myself to all the drugs. I had no peace. I couldn't eat, drink, or sleep for 25 days straight. My face started to deteriorate, my hair was falling out, and I couldn't see properly. It was demonic. I would hear many disgusting predictive voices and sounds all at the same time. I heard voices telling me demonic things like my uncle would commit suicide, and shortly after, he did. I would see my shoes and feet moving around by themselves, walking around in the room. The cabinet

> Roma said with tears streaming down her face, "Abuela looked me right into my eyes and said, 'I love you.'"

doors would open, and things would come out of them. Weird things were dragging up the stairs. I went out and slept on the streets because I wanted to get away from the unwelcome demons in my home.

I contemplated suicide many times. I forced myself to stay awake because the things I saw in my sleep were worse than things I was seeing when I was awake. I would run away to the beach and try to get rid of the ugly creatures, but they followed me there. I was tormented day and night. I was desperately searching for a different life. I went to a Catholic church and told the people what I was experiencing, but they didn't believe me.

I went home exhausted, hopeless, and crying. I couldn't contain myself any longer and went crazy, violently breaking everything with a baseball bat. I broke windows and screamed at the top of my lungs out of desperation and despair. The one window I broke, I looked through and I saw a dead person. I went downstairs to find a doctor who was renting the rooms. I held a pistol to him asking what happened to the man and what was going on. The police came and took me to prison. I was put in a corner prison cell at four in the afternoon. I didn't know what to do, so I sat and stared at the wall. I was being tormented in my mind by too many things. At 8:00 PM that night, there was a man who came into the prison and was crying. He shifted from sobbing and started yelling scripture verses from Proverbs and John.

He continued all night long and, in the morning, when I looked over, I saw a well-dressed man. He turned to me and said, "God has not forgotten you; you are His child, His daughter. He loves you." He asked if I wanted anything, and I said water. He left me a water bottle and pop in the office. I was in jail for three days. During my time there, the torment started to cease. It was a welcome relief.

My dad came and picked me up and took me into a Christian rehabilitation center. The pastor from the rehab center asked me if I knew why I was there. "No", I said. He repeated the exact same thing as the man in prison. "God has not forgotten you; you are His child, His daughter. He loves you." I stayed at the rehab center for five months. I was treated well and then it unexpectedly changed. I was disciplined for being rebellious and then I was treated poorly from that point forward. I was neglected, and they restricted my food to a small amount, stuffing me in a room the size of a stall.

My family from the U.S., who was paying for me to be in rehab, had forgotten about me. There was nobody to advocate for me. One day, I was at my end and could no longer handle living at the center. I told the guard to let me leave or I would escape. The office called my dad and he said he would put me back into jail if I left. I told my dad I loved him, but I knew I had to leave. The rehab worker told me if I left, I would have to leave all my clothing, the keys to my rental, everything. I left with the shoes on my feet and the clothing I was wearing.

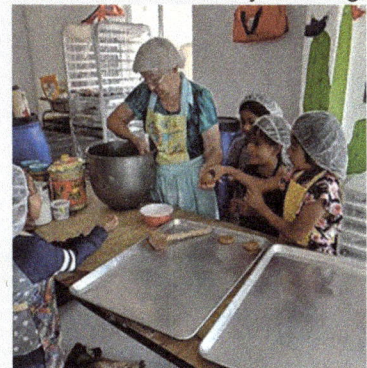

I walked hastily towards the highway and when I got to the road there was a man waiting for a vehicle to take him to church. He asked me if I would go with him once the car arrived. I said sure because my only other plan was to walk back to Vicente Guerrero and get into my rental; riding with him would get me closer to where I was going.

The service touched my heart in a way I had never experienced. I ended up staying for both church services. After the service, I talked to the pastor, and he told me about a place called Mujeres Nuevo Comienzo. I arrived at MNC later that day. Abuela greeted me. I was at the lowest of my lows. I had been in the ugliest places and used to be a drug dealer. Despite all of that, she drew me into her arms and told me how loved I was. I thought I didn't deserve anything good in life because I had made such poor, destructive decisions.

My life has changed here. I am learning to love and soften and show the women and people around me I care for them and love them. My hope, my dream is to be a mother for my son again. I want to be responsible and have a safe and good home where there is peace and no drugs. I am working towards those right now. I am working at a grocery store in the town. Previously, I believed I would be locked up for the rest of my life. I have been clean from drugs for one year and now I have hope believing one day I will have a life with my son.

Author's Note:

A volunteer at MNC says Roma has seen God and has seen the devil. She knows good, and she knows evil. Roma chose to go back to drugs. She was at MNC for seven months. She started working off-site at four months, and after three months of working, she tested positive for drugs and left. It is unknown where she is now.

Shabbat White Bread

Enjoyed weekly on Fridays when all the staff and residents share a meal together before a weekend of rest.

Ingredients:

⅓ cup oil of choice
3 cups warm water
⅓ cup sugar

1 tbsp instant yeast
8 cups all-purpose flour
1 egg white

Directions:

Preheat the oven to 350°F.

In a large mixing bowl place 3 cups warm water, ⅓ cup sugar, and 1 tbsp yeast.

Allow the yeast to rise for approximately 5 minutes.

Once yeast has started to rise, add the remaining ingredients, and mix with a bread hook for 5 minutes or hand knead for 10 minutes.

Once mixed very well, place plastic wrap over the dough and allow it to rise for 1½ hours until it has doubled in size.

Flour a clean surface and put the dough onto the surface. Cut it into equal pieces (approximately 2 cups dough for each piece).

Roll each piece into a long string. You want them to be about 1 inch thick.

Repeat until all your pieces are rolled out. Take three pieces and braid them together and pinch at either end. Repeat until you use all your strips.

Crack one egg into a small bowl and separate the whites and yolks. Brush the egg whites onto the bread. Grease a baking sheet and set the bread onto it. Place the tray in the oven and cook for 35 minutes or until the bread is golden brown. Enjoy with honey and butter.

Now what?

Now what?

It can be a dark and hopeless world for many. God has done some incredible and miraculous things at MNC. There is still a lot of work to do. Trafficking is increasing worldwide. Abuse is also increasing, and there are few facilities available that — like MNC — allow women to bring their children with them. One of the women who was interviewed for her testimony said she traveled for three days across Mexico to get to Vicente Guerrero because there was no other facility specific to rescuing women from abuse and trafficking where she could keep her children with her.

As you have read through the testimonies, you've seen many of the ladies saying, "Thank you!" They truly appreciate all the help and support that made it possible for them to have a better chance in life.

You may wonder how you can help these ladies and the ones to come.

Go volunteer at the mission. Being there and helping serve is a life-changing experience for you and the people there.

Encourage others to donate time, prayers, and resources.

Buy this book as a gift for someone.

Send items on their wish list sent in the monthly newsletter.

Pray.

The intent of this book is to provide another form of income for Mujeres Nuevo Comienzo as well as awareness of needs in this world. The publisher has donated their resources to this project as well as both authors and all contributors. There are many more lives to help.

Daily Prayer List:

- Women and children (past, current, and future residents) and their families
- Protection
- Health and safety
- Finances, resources, and donations
- Healing
- Volunteers and staff
- The land, buildings, automobiles, garden, and animals.

When you see the operating costs, you might be surprised. What you are not seeing is the amazing way $10,000 stretches. Thankfully, there are community supporters who provide what they can as well. Local farms donate leftover fruits and vegetables, and some donate commodities like oil, beans, and pasta. These staples give the residents a hearty pantry from which to make meals. Other donations are those of labor; groups may come and spend time fixing existing structures or building new structures to meet needs on the property.

Some months have lower costs, some months have much higher costs. Some months, the donations are quite low — around $2,000 — and do not cover the expenses, in and other months, a contributor holds a huge fundraiser and raises $50,000 so there is enough plus some to cover special projects. Dorothy has a vision to extend the reach and services of MNC: she wants to hire more staff so they can better support the ministry. There are also many unfinished projects needing to be funded. There are buildings needing to be finished, floors with bare concrete that need covering, and new buildings needing to be added, and the list of needs is as varied as the women who come to the shelter.

As well as current needs, unexpected expenses come up just as they do for us at home: cars break down, unplanned medical expenses pop up, natural disasters occur, equipment and appliances break, and tools need to be replaced.

"Why should I donate?"

Giving not only helps fill a financial void for the mission, but giving also fills the giver's heart and the recipient's heart. Giving and serving others creates a triple power effect by releasing oxytocin, dopamine, and serotonin. An article from the New York Times noted volunteering, donating money, or even just thinking about donating money can release feel-good brain chemicals and activate the pleasure center part of the brain. Additionally, givers also showed lower levels of the stress hormone, cortisol, by donating time or money.

More than the impact on ourselves, there are some other things to consider. Money is an important asset. It is the "bartering" system to accomplish things. Zig Ziglar said "Money isn't the most important thing in life, but it is relatively close to air on the got-to-have it scale." Ziglar was a great Christian man who used the talents God gave him to sow into the lives around him, impacting millions, and the ripple effect continues to this day. He trusted God with what he was blessed with. The lesson is similar for all of us: we all make a ripple effect; when we choose to relinquish something important to us to help others, the blessings pouring back in our own life are immeasurable. Choosing to give is choosing to be part of the transformation journey of others. Prayer and faith in God to help the ministry grow and thrive are essential to the success of MNC. Money to buy materials, food, supplies, and have resources needed for the ministry to flourish is important, but prayer and faith moves the hand of God and releases His blessings upon earth.

> Trust God from the bottom of your heart; don't try to figure out everything on your own. Listen for God's voice in everything you do, everywhere you go; he's the one who will keep you on track. 9 Honor God with everything you own; give him the first and the best. Donating money, time, and or talent is a way to live out.
>
> Proverbs 3:5, 6, 9 (MSG)

Money is one of the things we hold close to our hearts because we know the power it provides for us to live. When we give it to others, we are giving precious hope to those needing the power as well. MNC is trustworthy and uses every penny they have to help a life.

You've seen in the testimonies how many lives have changed because others have given to the ministry. What we may not live to see is the depth and width of impact we are making on a community by supporting this mission. It isn't just giving dollars; it is giving part of what powers us, to power them. We're choosing to say yes to the hope and changed lives.

Follow along on social media and sign up for Dorothy's newsletters to stay up to date. Even if the only resource you can provide is prayer, then pray, and be blessed in the knowledge God is listening and working. Prayers are always needed. Prayer can move mountains.

Thank you so much for purchasing this book, supporting the mission of helping hurting women and children, and being part of their journey. ALL of the proceeds from this book go to the ministry.

For more information about the ministry and donating visit: https://www.mncfreshstart.org/

Office: 616-115-7777

Email: nuevocomienzoac@gmail.com

Canada: https://www.mncfreshstart.org/canadian-donations

United States: https://www.mncfreshstart.org/us-donations

"We make a living by what we get,
but we make a life by what we give."

_____

Winston Churchill

About The Authors

Emily Giesbrecht, a native of Fort St. John, Canada, is a dedicated full-time student pursuing a future as a social service worker. Raised in the natural beauty of British Columbia, she finds joy in hiking, swimming, and camping, while her family holds a special place in her heart. Her ultimate dream is to work with children dealing with behavioral challenges, combining her passion for helping others with her studies. Emily's journey is a testament to her commitment to making a positive impact on the lives of those in need.

Lisa Costa, an Idaho native with a humble upbringing in a small town, now pursues a doctorate after being inspired by a teacher to embrace education. With over 15 years in education and seven years as a high school teacher, she has garnered state and national accolades, including the FCCLA Hall of Fame. Holding leadership certifications, such as Ziglar Choose to Win Coach, Lisa passionately guides others to discover their superpower. Committed to making a positive impact, she volunteers locally and abroad, enhancing lives. Cherishing the quote, "The two most important days of your life are the day you were born and the day you find out why," Lisa values family and friends, savoring life's moments.

Acknowledgements

Thank you to all supporters!

Thank you to Susie, Jorge, Paul, Jerry, and so many community constants who assist and those whose names I don't know.

To the many, many who have volunteered a few hours or a few years at MNC.

Thank you to those who give monthly support or send gifts throughout the year.

Thank you to those who helped bring this book to the shelf! Many of you spent many hours helping to edit and give feedback to help this book be the most incredible testimony and cookbook it could be.

Thank you to contributors Paul, Jorge, Susie, Daryle, Carol, Jen, Kirstin, April, Haley, Sarah, Liberty, Kylie, Mike, Linda, Leonard, Gwen, Teresa, Kenzi, Claire, and the Launch Committee.

Thank you to Performance Publishing for your incredible donation to get this book in the hands of many and help continue the support of healing for many years to come.

Thank you to Marcos Lee for taking pictures of many recipes featured in this book.

I believe many of us will never know the true impact we have had but trust in knowing another family is experiencing a better life because we chose to join the journey.

There are so many who have left footprints on Mujeres Nuevo Comienzo. Some are still there volunteering and others are still involved through prayer and support.

And you – thank you for joining the journey by simply buying this book.

Notes

Brown, E. L.Ac. DACM. (2020, February 15). Tissue memory – how emotional trauma gets trapped in the body. Updated: August 21, 2020. [The Alchemy Project]. https://www.the-alchemy-project.com/post/tissue-memory- how-emotional-trauma-gets-trapped-in-the-body

Front Psychol. 2010; 1: 246.Published online 2011 Jan 31. Childhood Trauma and Chronic Illness in Adulthood: Mental Health and Socioeconomic Status as Explanatory Factors and Buffers

Mock, S. E., & Arai, S. M. (2002). Child Illiteracy in America: Statistics, Facts, and Resources. Regis College. https://pubmed.ncbi.nlm.nih.gov/?term=Mock%20SE%5BAuthor%5D

Parker-Pope, T. (2020, April 9). The Science of Helping Out. New York Times. https://www.nytimes.com/2020/04/09/well/mind/coronavirus-resilience-psychology-anxiety-stress-volunteering.html

Index